P9-DXJ-487

AMERICAN

LOCOMOTIVES

IN HISTORIC PHOTOGRAPHS

1858 to 1949

✦

RON ZIEL

DOVER PUBLICATIONS, INC.
NEW YORK

To my father, Roland W. Ziel, who
introduced me to working steam locomotives
at a very early and impressionable age.

Picture Credits

Except as noted, all photographs are from the
William A. Rogers Collection, now part of
the Hayward Cirker Collection.

Copyright © 1993 by Ron Ziel.
All rights reserved under Pan American and International Copyright Conventions.

Published in Canada by General Publishing Company, Ltd., 30 Lesmill Road,
Don Mills, Toronto, Ontario.
Published in the United Kingdom by Constable and Company, Ltd., 3 The
Lanchesters, 162–164 Fulham Palace Road, London W6 9ER.

American Locomotives in Historic Photographs: 1858 to 1949 is a new work, first
published by Dover Publications, Inc., in 1993.

Manufactured in the United States of America
Dover Publications, Inc., 31 East 2nd Street, Mineola, N.Y. 11501

Book design by Carol Belanger Grafton

Library of Congress Cataloging-in-Publication Data

Ziel, Ron, 1939–
    American locomotives in historic photographs : 1858 to 1949 / Ron Ziel.
        p.   cm.
    Includes index.
    ISBN 0-486-27393-8 (pbk.)
    1. Locomotives—United States—Pictorial works.   I. Title.
TJ603.2.Z53   1993
625.2'6'0973—dc20   92-22927
                                                                                          CIP

CONTENTS

INTRODUCTION

The early development of the Industrial Revolution, which began in England during the mid-eighteenth century, was severely limited by the lack of a means of transporting raw materials and finished goods for long distances over land. Prior to this time, virtually every community was self-sufficient, with local artisans and mechanics supplying all but the most complex of devices necessary for living in a world considerably less complicated than today's. The earliest railways began appearing in the coal-mining areas of Britain when it was discovered that horses could haul much heavier loads if the wagons were equipped with flanged wheels that rode on wood or iron rails, rather than dirt (or mud) roads. By the year 1800, steam had been harnessed to power low-pressure pumps to clear water from the mine shafts, and even a few rudimentary steam-powered vehicles were being tested.

Leading industrialists, government officials and freight forwarders soon realized that if a mobile steam-powered engine could be married to the flanged wheel, a "brigade of wagons" could be coupled behind and the problem of distribution of commodities and people would be solved. Virtually without exception, early industry developed along waterways—rivers and canals—to provide both cheap mass transportation and power (in the form of water wheels) to the fledgling mills and foundries. Towns away from navigable waterways saw in the possibility of railways a chance to become industrialized while greatly expanding the markets for their agricultural and mineral produce as well. Indeed, the common wisdom of railroad promoters early in the nineteenth century was that canals and rivers would remain the primary arteries of transport, with railways merely connecting them, so long-distance commerce would still move primarily over water, despite the time and expense of transferring cargo from railway cars to barges and back to cars along the way. By the 1840s, the railroads had already subordinated the canals more rapidly than had ever been foreseen, much as the motor vehicle would eclipse the horse less than a century later.

The basic steam engine had already provided marine power, and even a small vertical boiler soon proved vastly superior, in terms of constant output and reliability, than wind or water had ever been. Wherever the railroads were laid down, factories and mills powered by steam soon followed. Well before the mid-nineteenth century, the Industrial Revolution was in full motion, riding the rails behind diminutive—but powerful—four-, six-, and eight-wheel steam locomotives.

With the coming of cheap, fast and reliable rail transport, the lives of ordinary people in both rural and urban areas underwent a radical change, unmatched in human history for its swiftness and finality. The primary effect was the breakdown of isolation in all facets of life: economic, social and cultural. The ages-old suspicion of strangers and alien ideas began to modify as hordes of both began arriving on the steam cars. Exotic goods and artworks, formerly available only to the small-minority aristocracy, soon were seen in the homes of local business leaders and, in time, their plant managers and, by the dawn of the twentieth century, even some of their workers.

The most profound influence of the early railways, however, was their ability to move masses of people. Before the railroads, a common person—a farmer or laborer, even a tradesman—if he lived a hundred miles from a large city, could expect to visit that city but once or twice in his lifetime, and the journey would take two or three days each way by stagecoach. A steam train made the same journey in about four hours, for less cost, and with a much smoother ride and far less inconvenience and danger. Individual mobility, to a degree unheard of in all previous human history, was the primary and vital contribution of the railway. The twentieth-century revolutions in personal transport brought first by the automobile and later by the airplane, while significant, in no way compared to those of the steam railways and the steamship.

By 1900, the railroads were thoroughly established worldwide as the lord of land transport, carrying ninety percent of all intercity freight and almost all passengers. Steam-locomotive technology, especially in the United States, was developing at an impressive rate, with ever larger, heavier and more powerful machines coming into routine use. In the 1920s, the full development potential of the reciprocating steam locomotive was nearly attained, even as the popularity of electric traction was making its mark and the diesel was in its infancy. Even before World War II, the diesel had successfully challenged the supremacy of steam in America and after the war it took but a decade for U.S. railroads to go from ninety percent steam to ninety percent diesel; in 1960 the last main-line steam engines were retired. Worldwide, steam lasted longer, but by the 1990s, few regular-service steam locomotives still survived, with a few in eastern Europe, Africa and South America, as well as on the Pacific rim. Only India, with about four thousand active steamers and China, with an estimated nine thousand, still field large numbers of steam engines in the final decade of the twentieth century. Indeed, China mass-produced main-line steam until 1989 and continued to turn out smaller industrial and forestry engines into the 1990s, the last country in the world to do so.

Hundreds of thousands—perhaps millions—of photographs were made of steam locomotives during the century and a half that they ruled the high iron, and many more are being added to the archives each year as thousands of railway enthusiasts turn out to make still pictures, movies, videos and sound recordings of preserved steam engines that still see occasional service powering special excursion trains. Although no photographs were made during the earliest years of railroads and few prior to the 1860s, it can be said that photography and railroading developed concurrently. Since the railways were, technologically, the Space Shuttle of their day, the intense interest of the general public in railways saw both free-lance and company photographers focusing their big view cameras on the railroad scene when both technologies were still relatively new.

Unfortunately, however, the further back in time historians research locomotives, the fewer photographs are found to have survived, the result of the usual ravages of time: carelessness, ignorance of historical importance, fires, floods and wars, the fragility of thin glass-plate negatives and other causes. Ofttimes an important old photograph survives only as a third-generation copy negative, devoid of most detail. The result of all this is that there exist few good-quality photos of locomotives built before 1890. Occasionally, however, a rare collection will surface, adding new knowledge to that provided by the sparse archives of the earlier generations of steam power. Such was the case of the compilation of Mr. William A. Rogers of Michigan, who accumulated builders' photographs of loco-

motives, acquiring many older and more unusual ones when they were still available to persistent aficionados. His extensive collection covered most of the history of steam, from the Civil War until the cessation of domestic commercial steam production in 1949. Fortunately, the publisher of this volume managed to acquire the Rogers Collection at auction some years ago and, after storing it with the idea of perhaps publishing the photographs in a book eventually, he asked me for my

thoughts on the matter. Initially skeptical, I agreed to come and look over the collection. The preponderance of nineteenth-century material was indeed impressive, for while photographs of many locomotives built during that era were taken late in the engines' careers (twenty to sixty years after they rolled out of the factory), these were unusual, for they showed the engines *as built*. Historically, this is extremely important, for, a decade or more after a locomotive came from the erecting shop, re-buildings and new appliances (air compressors, injectors and, later, superheaters and electrical systems) often left little of the locomotive's original appearance. Indeed, the renowned *General* of Civil War fame, built in 1855 and returned to active service during the centennial of that conflict, is estimated to retain but a ton or so of the original engine! Unlike a postage stamp, sculpture or even an antique toy train, an ancient building or piece of machinery, particularly a transportation vehicle such as an automobile or locomotive, can be almost totally renewed over time and still be considered the genuine item—provided that it is restored to a specific time period of its history.

All historians have visited automotive or aviation museums and seen a photo of the rusted frame of a 1904 Oldsmobile or a World War I Sopwith Camel fighter mounted next to the factory-new restoration; just five to twenty percent of the original remains! On locomotives this phenomenon is often documented on the machine itself. Removable parts were usually stamped with the road number of the engine, but items were often interchanged, particularly late in the career of a locomotive, when parts could be removed from retired sisters, saving the cost of fabricating replacements. Preserved Long Island Rail Road no. 39 is a good example. This locomotive has one six-ton pair of driving wheels from no. 40, a casting from no. 28 and her entire tender from no. 46! Still she is considered to be the complete and original Pennsylvania Railroad–designed G-5s, built in the P.R.R. Altoona Shops in June 1929.

From a photographic point of view, the pictures in the Rogers Collection are from a very exacting and disciplined school, well known to all railway historians as that of "builder portraits." Almost as soon as commercial photography—using collodion wet plates that had to be coated with emulsion, immediately exposed and then developed on the spot—became practicable in the 1850s, locomotive builders began keeping a photographic record of their handiworks. Initially, the builder would hire a local photographer, but as the railroads matured and some larger companies were turning out as many as ten locomotives *a day*, they acquired their own photo departments. Customarily, one engine from each order was selected for the "official portrait." If there was just one locomotive in the order, it was photographed; if there were a hundred, one—usually, but not always, the first—was selected for the honor.

Although the photos originally varied in angle from straight side views to almost frontal shots, there eventually evolved a sort of "standard format": views that were mostly from the side, but also partly from the front, with the driving rods in the lowest position and no escaping steam or smoke; all were taken in low sunlight or on a cloudy day. While some of the earlier builder photos showed engines minus their tenders, by the 1870s the tender was almost always included. Often, the side to be photographed (usually the right side) was painted a flat gray, and even numbered and lettered, then, as soon as the photographs were taken, returned to the paint shop to receive the traditional glossy black finish. Even with the

perfection of color photography in the late 1930s, builder photos were always done in black and white. A few colorful streamlined locomotives were photographed in color at the factory, but that was only done "unofficially" when the photographer felt that the appearance of the locomotive warranted the effort.

In addition to forming a record of the engines built, these portraits were of customer-relations value, with sturdily framed prints, covered with glass, being presented to high officials of the railroad to hang in their offices. Of course, the locomotive producers also had many photographs made of the erecting process, showing the various departments, boiler shops, frame jigs, wheel lathes, drop forges, tender shops and, finally, the erecting floor with its myriad of activities, including huge locomotives hanging from the slender cables of overhead traveling cranes. Like most other relics associated with the age of steam railroading, builder photos—especially in the original company frames—are valuable collector's items today.

While most books that celebrate the now virtually extinct machine that made the Industrial Revolution and modern society possible, concentrate on dramatic, smoky action photos, the present book shows these machines appearing uncharacteristically lifeless. Yet, up until the 1880s, action had been virtually impossible to photograph, because slow film emulsions required exposures of a duration too long to "freeze" the motion, resulting in a lack of action in all photos taken before that time. Even early railroad-historian photographers were influenced by the requirements of the builder portrait—only they called it the "roster" shot—going

through great lengths, either in early morning or late afternoon, to get the engine positioned just right, with rods down, no background and nary a wisp of escaping steam. This school of photography exists even today, in the diesel age, with an additional caveat: the slide has to be an original Kodachrome and processed by Kodak. And no exceptions!

The early decades of railroading saw much experimentation, and many unusual—even downright weird—locomotives were built. Some of the strangest turned out to be very successful when used in a specialized service. Many are shown here. As the locomotive industry matured in America (as well as England, Germany, France, Japan and other industrial nations), builders developed a lucrative export trade. Sometimes American manufacturers built engines that were identical with those used on U.S. roads; often they erected them to plans supplied by the purchaser. The latter often closely resembled—indeed, some were indistinguishable from—foreign locomotives.

The collection assembled by the resolute William A. Rogers runs the gamut of builder photographs, and while the accent in this book will be on the oldest and rarest locomotives, the modern are also represented, to show how highly developed the American steam locomotive had become prior to dieselization. Unfortunately, little is known of the histories of many of the locomotives once the factories delivered them to the purchasers. The main shortcoming of the Rogers Collection lies in the fact that the few notes accompanying the pictures are often totally inaccurate (he had the construction date of one class of engine off by almost forty years!) so they were not used by the author. Most important, the present collection affords a rare and privileged look back at steam power in its earlier, formative years, right up to its demise, through an often rigid, standardized school of photography. Standardization, however, offers the best basis for comparison for those who wish to learn a bit of the development of a subject. If this book manages to convey a sense of that development, it will have succeeded in its purpose.

RON ZIEL

Water Mill, New York, U.S.A.
January 1991

AMERICAN
LOCOMOTIVES
IN HISTORIC PHOTOGRAPHS

One of the earliest builder photographs is also of a primeval export locomotive: a diminutive narrow-gauge 0–4–0 tank engine that was built for the government of Spain in 1858. The tapered balloon stack is a good indication of its age, for this style was pretty well outdated by 1860. A most basic locomotive, *España* was equipped with an early injector just forward of the cab, as well as a crosshead-mounted water pump, and the steam dome was placed above the firebox, inside the cab, with safety valve and whistle protruding through the roof.

1

"España"

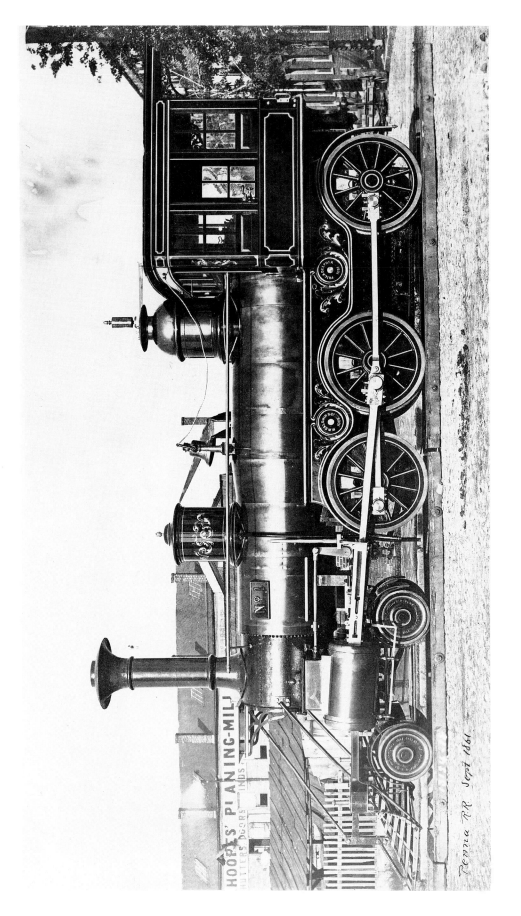

Penna P.R. Sept 1861

2
Pennsylvania Railroad No. 1

By 1860, the 4–6–0 ten-wheeler locomotive, larger and more powerful than the 4–4–0, or "American Standard," type, was being built, initially as a heavy (for that time) freight engine. With no. 1 of the Pennsylvania Railroad, Mathias W. Baldwin's factory had already been well established, this being his 1,009th locomotive, which was turned out in September 1861, just a few months after the outbreak of the Civil War. Railroads often do not number their engines consecutively, so the P.R.R., which was chartered in 1846, had had at least one previous no. 1. A cast plate, usually of brass, was affixed to each side of a locomotive, giving the name of the builder, the serial number, the date of construction and, usually, the location of the foundry. Some early Baldwins, such as this one, had two plates, ornately displayed between the driving wheels: the front one said "M. W. Baldwin & Co. 1009"; the rear one, "Philadelphia 1861." The Baldwin Locomotive Works, as it was later known, went on to erect nearly 75,000 locomotives—including some very impressive diesels—before all production ceased in the 1950s.

Pennsylvania Railroad 0–6–0 no. 216 emerged from the erecting hall at Baldwin in August 1861 as a fearsome apparition of Gothic character, with its bulky components, massive smokestack, high-mounted canted cylinders and awkwardly positioned wheels. The box of a water cistern slung over the boiler and the massive dome scrunched up against the pin-striped cab did nothing to detract from the ungainly visage of this early switch engine. Certainly at this stage of development, the steam locomotive was still experiencing aesthetic growing pains. Within a decade, however, it would mature into an embodiment of elegance and refinement that in taste and proportion would rival the clipper ship and Federal architecture. Such details on no. 216 as the one-piece molded fender over the wheels, the wrought-iron bell cradle and the paint trim could only hint at the princely splendor of the typical steam locomotive later in the nineteenth century.

3

Pennsylvania Railroad No. 216

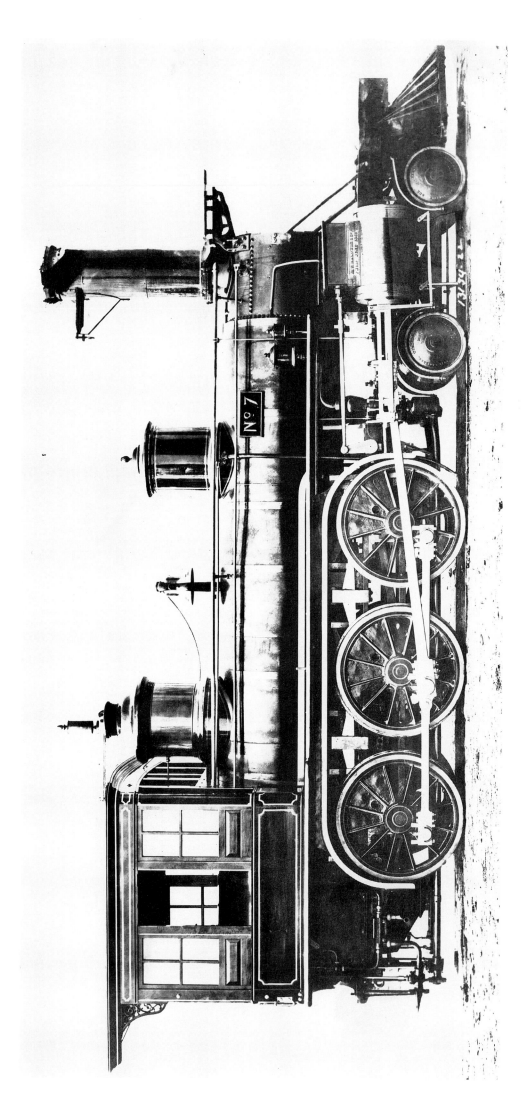

4

*Eastern
Pennsylvania
Railroad No. 7*

Baldwin's 1,114th locomotive was a utilitarian 4–6–0 built for the Eastern Pennsylvania Railroad in June 1862. Instead of mounting a cast plate itemizing the builder's information, that data was cast directly into the bottom of the valve chest above the cylinder. Locomotives of this period mounted enormous headlights on a platform directly in front of the smokestack, which housed a large reflector to magnify the weak oil flame that provided the illumination. Often, the railroad itself supplied the headlight—sometimes exquisitely decorated, including pastoral scenery or a portrait of the person for whom the machine was named—so many of the factory photos show engines devoid of the lamps. Barely three decades after the power of steam locomotives first proved practical as a successor to that of animals, engines such as no. 7 shown here had already attained a technological sophistication that was recognizable even in its gigantic descendants in the twentieth century.

5

*Union Pacific
Railroad No. 90*

A year and a month prior to the Golden Spike ceremony at Promontory Point, Utah Territory, on May 10, 1869, Baldwin completed a brutish 4–6–0, no. 90, for the Union Pacific. It would be a month before the ten-wheeler arrived on its owner's property in Omaha, Nebraska, and went to work hauling freight—much of it construction materials for the U.P.—to help complete the epic labor of the first transcontinental line. Typical of the 4–4–0s and 4–6–0s of its era, no. 90 had a wide space between the rear sets of driving wheels, to allow room for the firebox to be mounted between the axles. The biggest improvement in locomotive design occurred in the 1890s when trailing wheels enabled the firebox to be carried above the frame. This enabled fireboxes to be increased enormously in size (in both width and length) and ultimately resulted in the high-horsepower steam-generating boilers of the 1900s.

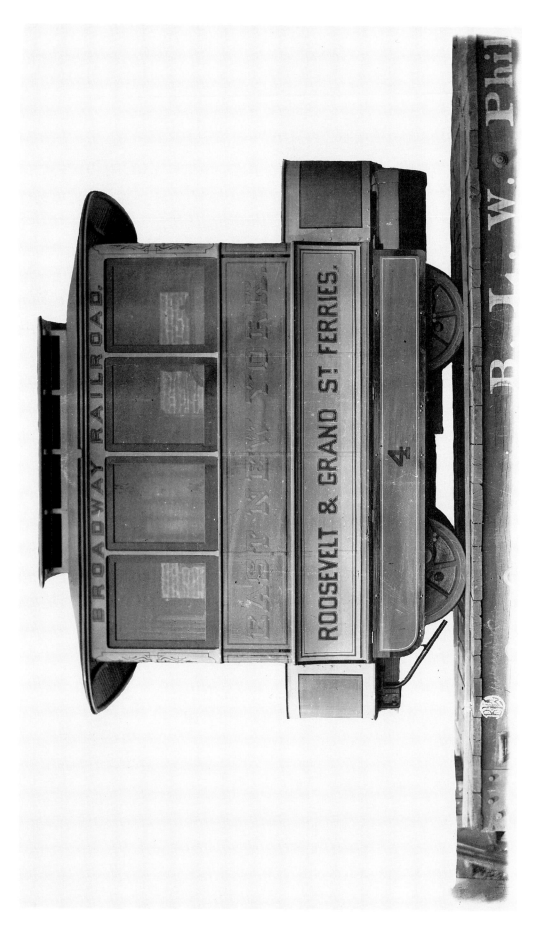

6

Broadway Railroad
No. 4

Street railways, utilizing horses to power small passenger cars, began to appear in American cities even prior to the War Between the States. Most of them retained equine energy until they were electrified, beginning in the 1890s, heralding the advent of the trolley or tram lines. The inherent economics and improved performance of steam on the railways soon became obvious to the horsecar line operators, but running steam locomotives down city streets presented problems. Hissing steam, oscillating, clanking machinery and belching smoke frightened horses and children, disturbed peaceful neighborhoods and blackened washlines. The solution was to hide the steam engine, to make it appear little different from the familiar cars it was replacing. The resulting steam cars, while never widely accepted in the United

States, were nevertheless to become a common sight in cities around the world, the last operating in Indonesia in the 1970s. Powered by diminutive wash boilers, the steam tram lines either used "dummy" locomotives decked out to resemble horsecars to pull a passenger car, or, in the larger versions, had a passenger compartment that shared the car with a partitioned-off boiler. Broadway Railroad no. 4 was of the former type. Built by Baldwin in 1868, it ran in the city of Brooklyn, New York, from the Roosevelt and Grand Street ferries on the East River, out to East New York. With a car body completely enclosing the locomotive—even the wheels were covered—the engine was indistinguishable from a small horsecar.

7

Chimbote Railway
"Emilia"

One of the most fascinating and affable of all the little inspection engines built for the use of company officials was the Chimbote Railway 2–2–4T, named *Emilia*, dating back to 1868. The boiler, with its incredibly slender diamond-capped stack, minuscule cylinders and tall domes, was entirely exposed, while the cab was extended back to include a completely separate compartment for the company "brass" to ride in style while inspecting the track and facilities. With wainscotted paneling, arched windows, clerestory roof, open rear platform and ornate gold-leaf trim, this was more than a mere locomotive—it was truly a masterpiece of art, in the highest sense of the term.

8

Chicago & North-Western Railway "Alexander Mitchell"

The Chicago & North-Western began building in the 1840s. Within twenty years it had pushed its rails westward into Sioux Indian territory, utilizing high-drivered 4–4–0s that were quite sizable for their time. Built in December 1869, the diamond-stack American named *Alexander Mitchell* is seen here posed outside of the Baldwin factory in low winter sunlight. About the only parts of these primeval steam locomotives of the 1860s that would remain virtually unchanged seventy years later were the bell and the builder's plate; each and every other component would undergo a metamorphosis in size, shape and technological improvement comparable to that experienced by all other forms of mechanical endeavor during that period.

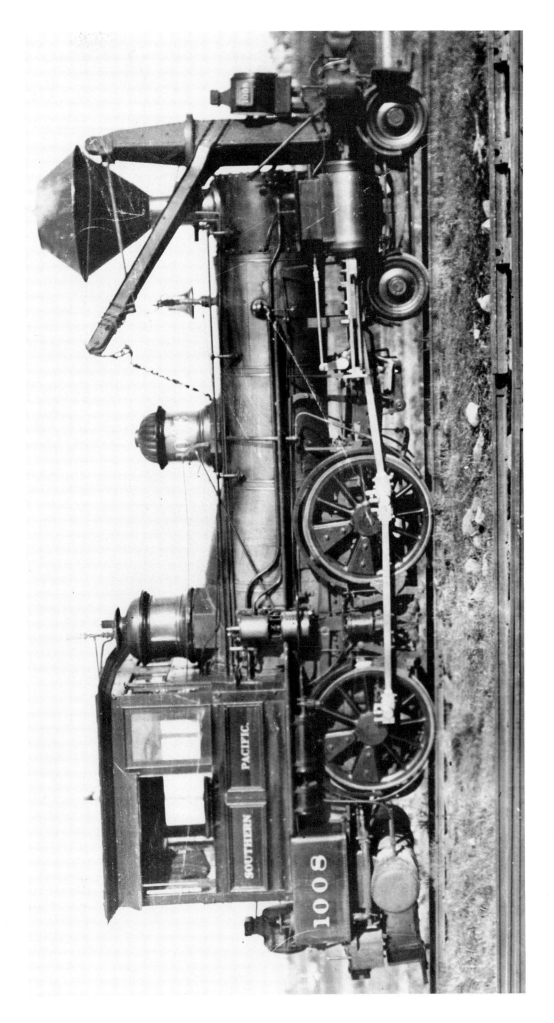

Another aesthetic calamity of an 1860s-era locomotive was Southern Pacific 4–4–0T no. 1008, which apparently began life as a conventional tender-equipped road engine, then was downgraded to work-train and switching service. This, in effect a "rebuilder" photograph, was taken upon the hapless machine's emergence from Espee's Sacramento Shops about 1890. With a cumbersome crane mounted on the pilot beam and tiny fifty-gallon-capacity water tanks under the cab, this engine could not wander far from the shops area. The fluted cap on the sandbox reveals that she was built by the Rogers Locomotive & Machine Works of Paterson, New Jersey, long regarded as having been perhaps the most quality-oriented of all American locomotive manufacturers—although she hardly looks it in this picture!

9
___

Southern Pacific
Railway No. 1008

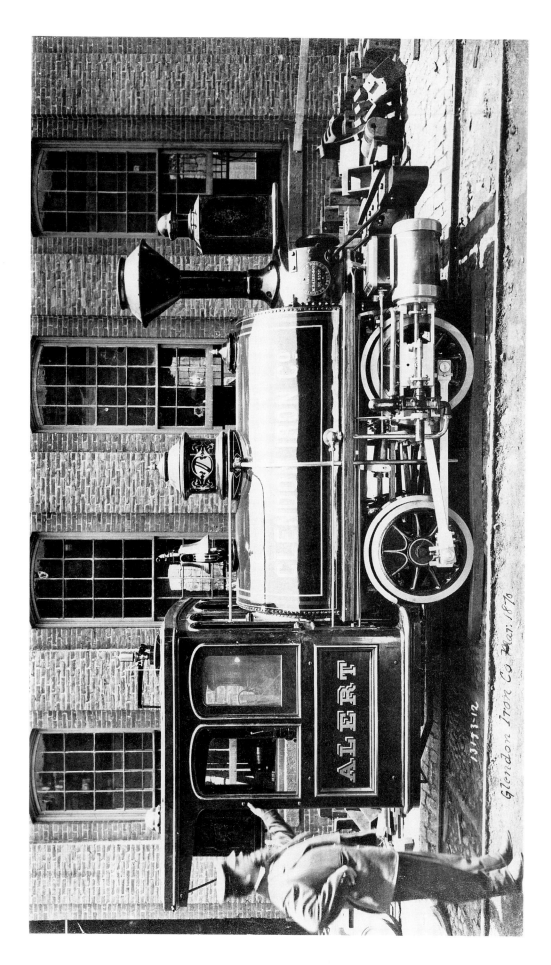

Glendon Iron Co. Mar: 1870

13.73-12

10

Glendon Iron Co.
"Alert"

Little narrow-gauge industrial tank engines have rarely been accorded more than passing acknowledgment by most railway historians, since they have been generally plain, awkward and even comical, compared to their larger main-line cousins. However, back in the second half of the nineteenth century, locomotive builders lavished great care on the construction of even the smallest and most obscure of engines. Probably, they felt—rightly so—that when their builder's plates were affixed to a machine, it became a representative of the firm's handiwork and worthy of the attention paid to all of the company's products. No doubt the tiny *Alert*, shown posed on a standard-gauge track with a timber supporting the near wheels (why the timber wasn't used

instead on the opposite side is a mystery), was rarely noticed by anyone but sweaty, grimy iron workers after she left the M. Baird & Company (a Baldwin subsidiary) works in March 1870. No matter, because the builders knew that for a few weeks at least, the officials of the Glendon Iron Co. would consider the tiny 0–4–0T to be an object of pride and a symbol of its prosperity, so she was outfitted with a paneled cab, shaded lettering, striping and a headlight fit for an engine four times her size! The gentleman wearing a jacket, celluloid collar and tie was probably a manager at Baird—or possibly the superintendent of the railroad operation at Glendon, down to witness the first firing-up of the brand-new saddle-tank switcher.

11

Ferro-Carril de Salaverry á Trujillo No. 9

Diminutive plantation engines, not too far removed in basic development from Ferro-Carril de Salaverry á Trujillo no. 9, named *Chocope*, were still active on the sugarcane lines of Cuba in the 1990s. Especially prominent on this little narrow-gauge 0–4–2T (of the 1885–1915 era) is the crosshead-mounted water pump, a forerunner of the modern injector, used to admit water to the boiler. Although such devices had disappeared from main-line power on most railroads by 1900, they may still be found on some of the smaller sugar-plantation engines in Cuba, the one country where railway technology may be observed still existing in various phases from 1870s steam to present-day diesel operations.

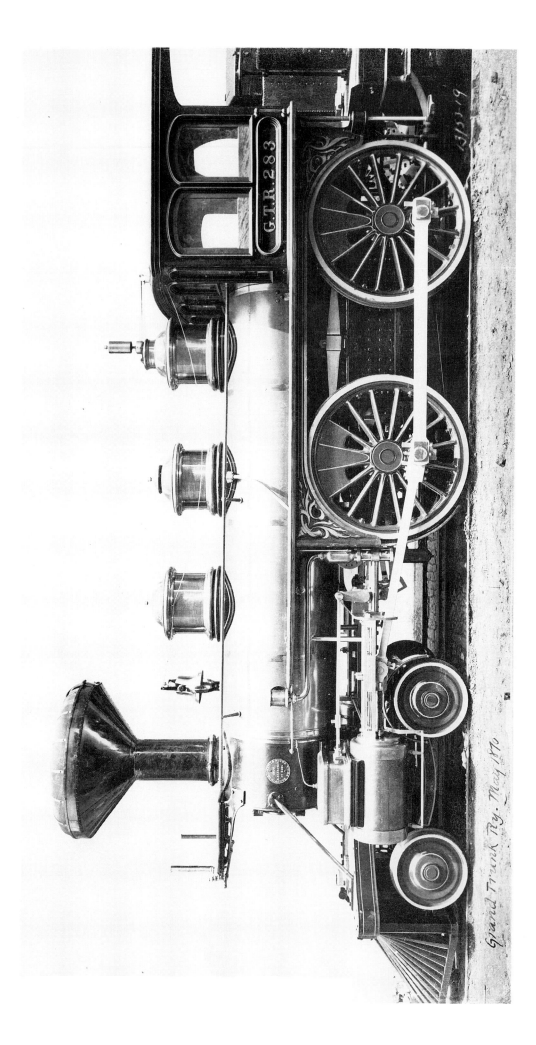

Grand Trunk Rly. May 1870

Grand Trunk Railway No. 283

Crowned with a mushroom-shaped spark-arrester stack, Grand Trunk Railway no. 283 was very representative of the dual-purpose 4–4–0 wood-burners built in the post–Civil War period, when the railroad building boom was heading for its zenith. Constructed in May of 1870, this engine, like many similar ones, could wheel passenger trains, lighter freights and—an important consideration in the 1865–90 period—construction trains. The 4–4–0 was by far the most popular type during the first half-century of railway expansion, with perhaps two-thirds of all road engines being of this American Standard type. It was not until well into the next century that the 2–8–0 would surpass it as the most numerous of locomotive types in the U.S.A.

13
Central Railroad of
New Jersey No. 125

Central Railroad of New Jersey 2–4–0 no. 125 was an early bidirectional suburban commuter locomotive, designed to pull fast, light trains, in forward or reverse. With the firebox centered above the rear driving axle, thereby raising the entire boiler, this 1871 engine was possessed of an unusually rakish and speedy look for its switcher size. The tiny four-wheel tender was equipped with a cowcatcher in back, allowing for reverse running. Most interestingly, no. 125 sported one of the earliest "all-weather" cabs, with the back enclosed to keep wind and precipitation out when the 2–4–0 was speeding backward. This feature is normally associated with twentieth-century locomotives operating in subzero climes, after crew comfort had become a management consideration. Concerns about derailing the tender probably restricted backward running to about thirty m.p.h., but, when galloping forward with a light train of two or three wooden coaches, this engine could maintain sixty with ease.

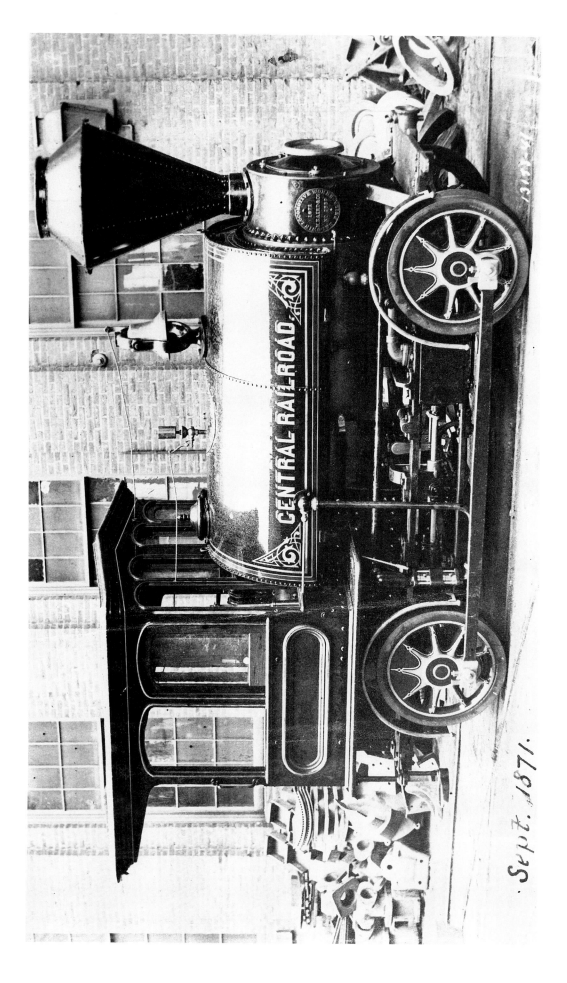

Sept. 1871.

14

Central Railroad

Few locomotives were more homely in appearance during the Victorian period than the odd shunter with just two axles positioned at the extreme ends of the frame. With crossheads and pistons mounted between the wheels and driving on axle cranks, the power was transmitted from one pair of wheels to the other by means of connecting rods that ran the length of the boiler. The enormous balloon stack almost balanced the Gothic cab that towered over the saddle tank. Posed among the clutter of engine parts, the little wood-burner, destined for the Central Railroad of Georgia, was on the track adjacent to Baldwin's erecting shop when new in September 1871.

15

Boston and Maine Railroad No. 47

The suburban tank engine saw extensive service in the United States and Canada for a century, with the last ones in the world still operating in India in the 1990s. Tank locomotives were very practical and economical for transporting passengers as well as freight and for shunting operations in areas where they were not required to do high-speed running over long distances. Because they had no separate tender and carried their water supply in a tank mounted alongside, or slung over, the boiler and their fuel in a bunker in the cab, they could run backward with equal ease, obviating the need to turn the engine at the end of a run. The additional weight of fuel and water on the frame of the locomotive also added to its adhesion, making it more powerful than tender engines of similar size. In passenger service, tank engines were used mostly on urban and suburban lines, from dinky little

four-wheelers on street and elevated railways in cities such as New York and Chicago, to 4–6–4Ts on the Central Railroad of New Jersey and 4–6–6Ts on the Boston and Maine, which saw service on suburban branch lines in the New York and Boston metropolitan areas. While the basic little 0–4–0T was the industrial and mining workhorse, deluxe examples, with taller driving wheels for increased speed, were conveying commuters as early as the 1850s. Boston and Maine no. 47, named *Achilles*, was built by Baldwin in January 1871. With its Gothic wooden cab, ornate striping and decoration and shaded lettering, set off by glistening brasswork, no. 47 hauled daily commuter runs with a style and grace not normally associated with such a mundane destiny.

16

Ashland Iron Co.
"Edward Patterson"

The Ashland Iron Company's simple little 0–4–0T, named *Edward Patterson*, was built in 1872 as a typical iron-mill shunter, little different from hundreds then in service and thousands to follow. This was the basic industrial and plantation locomotive that—a quarter-century later—the H. K. Porter Company, a Pittsburgh locomotive builder of renown, would still be promoting as being far superior to animal power. Indeed, even an engine so trivial in size, strength and sophistication as this one could be expected to replace an entire stable of mules or draft horses and their attendant grooms, hostlers and drivers, paying for itself within two years, as Porter claimed in its catalogues at the time.

17

Hilliard & Bailey's Lumber Railroad "Florida"

In the 1870s, during the post–Civil War Reconstruction era, with a vastly expanding and westward-moving population, there was an enormous demand for all manner of building materials in the United States, particularly lumber. The forest lands of the South were being rapidly exploited, and any logging operation with more than local distribution was sure to move timber to the sawmills by rail. The basic concept of the 0–4–2 tank engine, then being used on urban elevated lines, proved useful for industrial and mill switching as well. Hilliard & Bailey's Lumber Railroad 0–4–2T, named *Florida*, could have been plying the Kings County Elevated Railroad lines in Brooklyn just as easily as working log trains in the cypress swamps of the deep South. By the World I era, the little Baldwin 2–6–2 tender locomotive was rapidly gaining favor as the virtually standard logging engine in the forests of the former Confederacy.

18

Brooklyn, Bath & Coney Island Railroad "George"

The Brooklyn, Bath & Coney Island ran but a few miles, but it played a salient role in the urbanization of the New York metropolitan area. Originally it was built to carry crowds of Brooklyn residents to the distant, unspoiled beach at Coney Island; it was not long before year-round communities sprang up all along the right-of-way and the farmlands gave way to tract development. The locomotive *George* was a fine hybrid; while the car body covered the boiler, no attempt was made to conceal the running gear, and the diamond stack, whistle and bell protruded prominently above the roof. Built in 1871, this small 2–4–0T was used to haul passenger cars along city streets as well as on the railroad's own right-of-way. The B.B. & C.I. and several other similar operations were later absorbed into either the Long Island Rail Road or the New York City transit system.

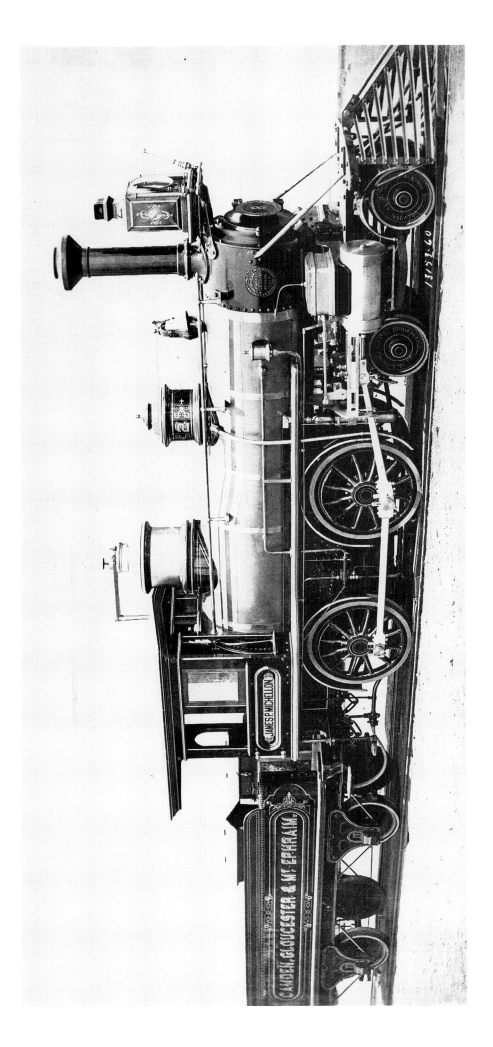

19

Camden, Gloucester & Mt. Ephraim Railroad No. 2

By 1874, when Baldwin built a low-drivered 4–4–0 named *James P. Michellon* for the Camden, Gloucester & Mt. Ephraim, in New Jersey, railroads were rapidly changing from wood to coal fuel. This change affected the appearance of engines like this, with its straight, slender stack and the humping of the boiler above its firebox. Wood as fuel was adequate even on much larger locomotives (the Russians substituted wood for coal in as many as eleven percent of their steamers during World War II, and the Finnish Railways ordered modern wood-burning 2–8–0s into the early 1950s), but the easier handling and increased energy produced by coal soon made it the dominant choice as fuel worldwide. Even after oil became popular, the most widely used fuel until the end of the steam era was those ubiquitous black diamonds. C.G. & Mt.E. no. 2 was serviced by a four-wheel tender with axles mounted under European-style pedestals beneath the outer frame.

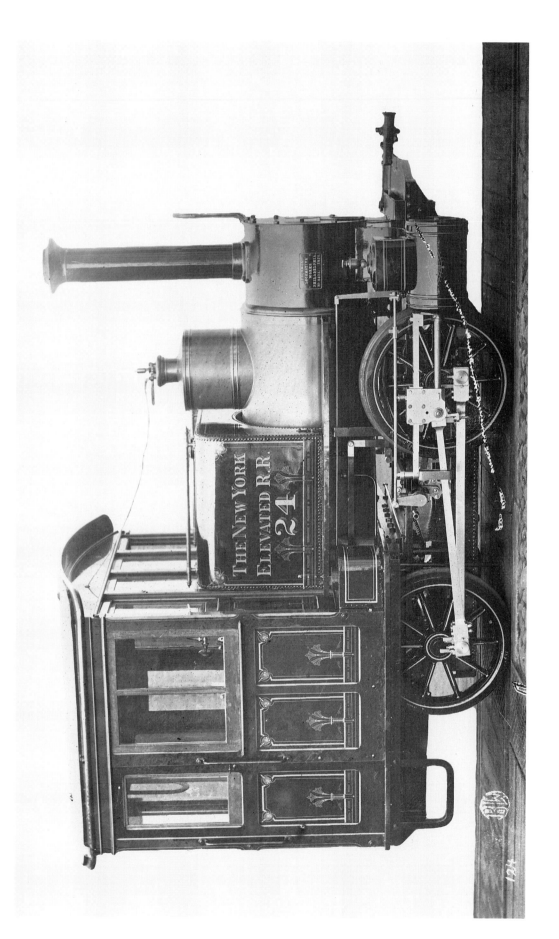

20

New York Elevated
Railroad No. 24

In the 1870s, the expansion of rapid transit in major cities such as New York meant that steam-powered railroads would be built above congested residential and commercial streets. Since the trains operated by the elevated railways consisted of two to six light wooden cars that had to screech to a stop, then rapidly accelerate every few blocks, the motive power was diminutive, carried a minimum of coal and water and had fairly large wheels. New York Elevated no. 24 was built in 1878 to run above the streets of Manhattan. In 1902–03, all of the "El" lines were electrified, retiring hundreds of these little teakettles within a span of a few months.

21

Long Island Rail Road No. 71

A very typical coal burner of 1879 was Long Island Rail Road no. 71, *Meteor,* the largest type of locomotive owned by that medium-size carrier at the time. The four-wheel pilot truck usually indicated that a locomotive was built for speed, since it was the primary function of those front wheels to guide the engine into curves. A two-wheel truck, or none at all, would necessarily restrict the top speed of an engine, which could more readily derail on curves. In the early days of railroading, however, the 4–4–0 became so universal a design that many lines used them almost exclusively as road power, even though a 2–6–0 would have been more practical in freight service. While most locomotive types could be placed in dual-service roles when necessary, just the 4–4–0 and later the 4–8–2, and finally the 4–8–4, were to become truly universal in their use, equally at ease with fast freights or heavy passenger consists.

22
Atchison, Topeka &
Santa Fe Railway
No. 91

The Atchison, Topeka & Santa Fe Railway, of legend and song, helped greatly in rolling back the frontier and in civilizing the West. Indeed, the proper young ladies that Fred Harvey brought to staff his many restaurants along the Santa Fe aided in the eventual taming of the vast wilderness, providing part of the stable, permanent society that came to supplant the nomadic cowpunchers, gamblers, prostitutes and other unsavory elements that had preceded them. In the 1870s, the route of the Santa Fe was the domain of chunky 4–4–0s like no. 91, and was still untamed, prone to attack by marauding Indians and delays by herds of buffalo numbering in the tens of thousands. The Southwest was still largely composed of vast territories of limitless potential that awaited the proper economic climate for orderly development and eventual statehood. Once the transcontinental railroads, such as the A.T. & S.F., were completed, no. 91 and other reliable American Standard locomotives moved the raw materials, merchandise, agricultural produce and people in such prodigious amounts, and with such unprecedented dispatch, that within twenty years civilization had advanced so far that it would be recognizable even today.

23
Cincinnati Inclined Plane Railway No. 1

An inclined-plane railroad was used to surmount steep grades in a relatively short distance, using various methods to power and lift the cars. In some instances, cars of equal weight were connected by a cable, one car ascending while the other descended on a parallel track. In other cases, a "dummy" engine—small and enclosed, such as this one—ran on a level or downgrade track beyond the incline, towing a cable fastened to the car. Cincinnati Inclined Plane Railway no. 1 (built ca. 1870–85) was almost a real-life version of the famed cartoon "Toonerville Trolley," especially with that dinky afterthought of a bell mounted on the back of the clerestory. Since the locomotive operated in a crowded urban setting, close to people and horses, for safety considerations its vertical boiler was camouflaged by a horsecar body, and panels almost totally obscured the running gear.

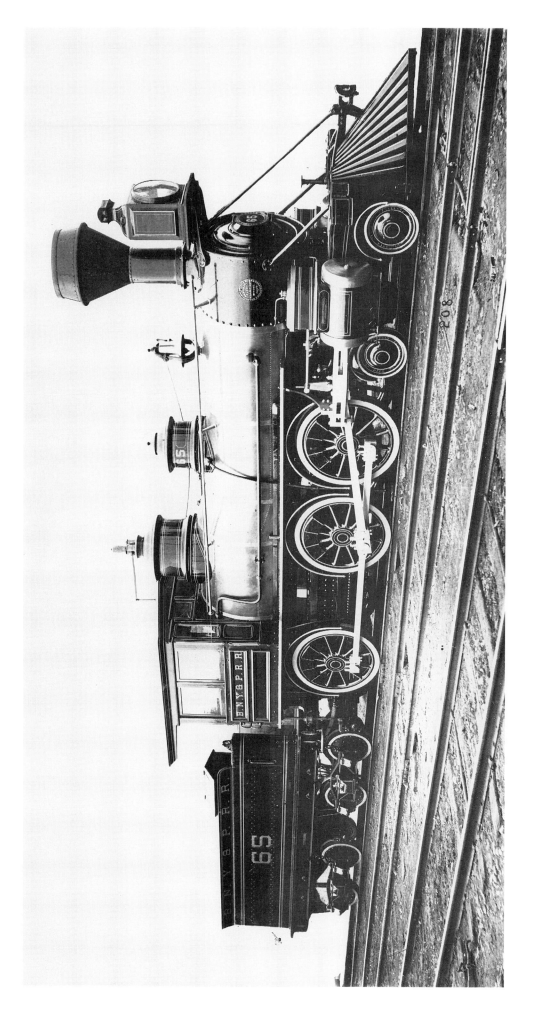

24

Boston, New York & Philadelphia Railroad No. 65

Among the thousands of locomotives turned out annually by American builders between 1880 and 1930, certain individual or series engines were so proportioned that they can truly be referred to as classics. Such was Boston, New York & Philadelphia 4–6–0 no. 65, an uncommonly beautiful example of the art at a time when handsome locomotives were the norm, rather than exceptional. From its pointed cowcatcher and combination balloon-and-diamond stack, to its striped tender, this 1883 ten-wheeler was every inch a pristine aristocrat; yet, with six driving wheels of moderate height, it was primarily intended for heavy freight chores. Little is known of its work or for how long no. 65 performed after Baldwin delivered her, but it can be assumed with certainty that the management and workers of the B.N.Y. & P. were as proud of this exquisite locomotive as the craftsmen who had erected her in Baldwin's huge Philadelphia complex.

25

Cia. E. de F.
Barão de
Araruama No. 3

As early as the 1830s, Great Britain had begun to export steam locomotives to the United States, but once Mathias Baldwin began to earn a reputation for building reliable engines, Americans, too, were able to establish a lucrative overseas market that would result in 20,000 or more steam locomotives being sent abroad in the century ending in 1953. Except for its squat, low driving wheels, 2–6–0, or "Mogul," type no. 3 (named *S. Francisco de Paula*) of the Cia. E. de F. Barão de Araruama, built for the Brazilian railroad in 1881, was a handsome duplicate, in every detail, of the finest domestic 2–6–0s of the time. Because of these early exports, American locomotive design practices greatly influenced the motive-power thinking of railways worldwide.

26
Saint Louis & San Francisco Railroad No. 2

By the 1880s, the slope-back tender had been devised for switching service, enabling the engine crew to look right down at the brakemen working behind. In the days before the invention of the automatic knuckle coupler, shunting operations were extremely dangerous, since brakemen had to stand between the cars while coupling up, and then do so with the use of finger-amputating link-and-pin couplers. Saint Louis & San Francisco 0–6–0 no. 2, built in 1881, complete with crosshead-mounted water pump, was a rather deluxe-model switcher, with its ornate striped domes and diamond stack, gray jacket, pinstriping and fenders above the wheels. Its diminutive tender, however, appears to have been the smallest thing ever to be mounted on two four-wheel trucks! It is doubtful that the water capacity of this tank could have been much more than a thousand gallons, but yard goats such as no. 2 were rarely to be found working more than a few hundred yards from a convenient water source. (For more on the term "yard goat," see photo 39.)

Ferrocarril Interoceánico No. 20

While the beauty inherent in steam locomotives designed in the last third of the nineteenth century is thoroughly ballyhooed in this book, there certainly were some aesthetically disastrous examples. Few can match the ungainly ugliness of the Ferrocarril Interoceánico Consolidations, typified by no. 20, built by Baldwin in 1881. Glossy sheen and striping cannot cover the misproportions that resulted in a steam dome that was as high as the undersized driving wheels and a fat, untapered sewer pipe of a boiler that seemed to bear down so heavily as to squash the frame and running gear right into the roadbed. Only the skyline and cab—when considered separately from the boiler—retained any artistic balance. Being an export locomotive, this ugly duckling fortunately did not get to offend the sensibilities of many Americans.

T. L. Hackney
Locomotive

Logging, mining and other backwoods industrial railroads had specialized locomotive requirements. These operations were characterized by very crude, ungraded rights-of-way, rough track and grades so steep that a standard rod-operated locomotive could barely get itself going, much less an entire train. Particularly in logging operations, which often saw track laid down for just a short period until the timber was cut, then moved in panels to another sector, the crudeness of track engineering was a marvel to behold, mostly for the total lack of such refinements as grading and bridges. If a stream was in the way, the tracks were often laid down one bank, across the bed and up the other side, with locomotives fording a two- or three-foot-deep raging current! Rod engines, with their rigid frames and machinery, frequently derailed or could often handle just one or two cars. In the early

1880s, Ephraim Shay designed a locomotive that was powered by vertically mounted cylinders driving a shaft along the right side that was geared to the wheels. Instantly successful, locomotives using his basic 1881 patents were built in the United States as late as 1945. In fact, the renowned Lima Locomotive Works of Lima, Ohio, which went on to become one of the "Big Three" American steam-locomotive builders and turned out what many experts considered the "Cadillacs" of U.S. motive power after 1920, went into business specifically to erect Shay's patent engines and, for several decades, that was their premier product. This rudimentary early Shay, constructed in 1885 for T. L. Hackney of Gilroy, West Virginia, is typical of the early vertical-boilered, geared locomotives that made the efficient cutting of vast tracts of timber possible.

29
Gilpin Tramway No. 181

Within two years of the construction of the basic vertical-boiler T. L. Hackney Shay, Lima turned out a two-foot-gauge Shay for the Gilpin Tramway in Colorado. Although small and probably weighing about twenty tons, it embodied all of the salient engineering features of the monstrous 162-ton standard-gauge Shay that would be built for the Western Maryland Railway in 1945.

Shown posed on the shop transfer table at Lima in 1887, this ornately striped little workhorse possessed a rakish flanged stack, bell and sandbox mounted on a standard horizontal locomotive boiler. Behind the engine, two workers are seen stretching a white cloth background for the photographer. Later, negatives

such as the one from which this print was made were invariably silhouetted with opaque retouching paint to completely obliterate the background. Apparently, this particular glass-plate was a duplicate of the one selected for retouching. Usually, such "dupes" were destroyed, but, fortunately, this one survived to show—more than a century later—how the standard "builder photo" was set up. Other designs of geared locomotives, most notably the Heisler and the Climax, were also produced and successfully run for many years, but the first one, the Shay, was to prove the most popular and the most lasting—as well as the most awkward and homely in appearance.

30

*Fort Bragg
Railroad Co. No. 2*

The highlights of some steam locomotives were so exaggerated that they were virtual caricatures of what may be considered "normal" features of the species. Such was Fort Bragg Railroad (North Carolina) no. 2, a Burnham, Parry & Williams graduate of 1887. This rather affable, pleasant little tank engine was obviously designed for the road rather than humble yard-goat duties. An enormous cowcatcher, with equally huge oil headlight and diamond stack, dwarfs her tiny boiler; indeed, even the standard builder's plate seems bigger than it should be. Further back, the saddle tank, domes and cab are well proportioned to the running gear of this 2–4–4T, but then there is that ostentatious backup light perched on the cab roof. Although a mite comical, no. 2 still exudes a rudimentary elegance and personality not found in some engines of considerably larger size and higher calling.

31

New York, New Haven & Hartford Railroad No. 149

By the end of the nineteenth century, the basic 4–4–0 passenger locomotive had evolved into a form that was to set the trends of development in the upcoming 1900s. Boilers and fireboxes had been greatly enlarged, with a corresponding increase in sustained steam-generating capacity. Vastly more powerful than the typical engine of just five years previously, chunky American Standards like New York, New Haven & Hartford no. 149 demonstrated for the first time the true potential of the steam locomotive, showing that it was possible to haul eight or ten cars over long distances at speeds of sixty to ninety miles per hour without the danger of running low on steam. With its clean lines and well-proportioned components, the 4–4–0 of the 1890s heralded the technological boom of the following decades.

32

Sinnemahoning
Valley Railroad
No. 2

In the 1880s, when more route-miles of new track were laid in the United States than in any other decade, the railroad industry was straining the productive capacity of the nation much as a major war effort would have done. Including double-tracking and sidings and yards, more than ten thousand miles of track were laid in some years, along with all of the bridges, tunnels, grading equipment and locomotives, cars, stations, shops and roundhouses necessary to make full use of the new railway plant. Coal and steel empires were being developed in a form recognizable even today, largely to supply the voracious needs of the rail industry. Locomotives were growing in size and power almost yearly and, by 1887, impressive 2–8–0s like Sinnemahoning Valley (Pennsylvania) no. 2 had become the heaviest freight movers. Engines such as this—burly and ungraceful—were the real workhorses that propelled the United States toward the attainment of Manifest Destiny and, beginning with the Spanish–American War, world-power status as well.

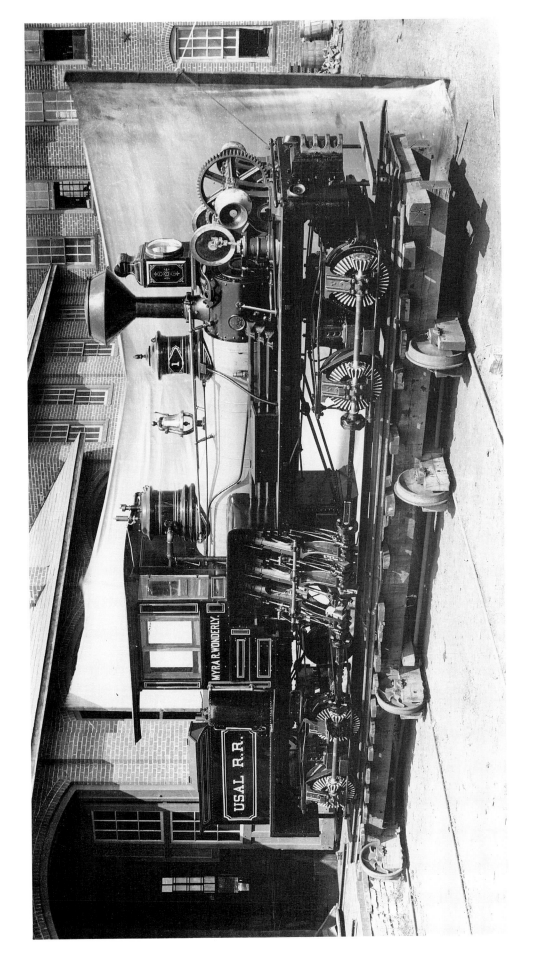

33

Usal Railroad
No. 1

Small industrial, mining and logging locomotives sometimes served in dual functions. One fascinating version (especially popular in England) was the crane engine, whereon a revolving boom crane was mounted above the cab or boiler, enabling the little loco to work either as a normal switch engine, moving cars about, or as a mobile crane, lifting heavy loads and carrying them around the factory yard or mill. Among other uses, some logging engines, such as narrow-gauge Shay no. 1 of the Usal Redwood Company in California, mounted geared winches on the front of the frame to drag fallen trees out of the woods and onto log cars. Driven by two vertically mounted cylinders in front of the smokebox, this mechanism could probably also power saws or other machinery through a leather-belt transmission. Since three vertical cylinders also powered the locomotive, it would seem that Lima, in its days as the sole builder of Shay-geared engines, totally shunned the conventional horizontal cylinder concept! Usal no. 1 was named *Myra R. Wonderly*—probably in honor of the wife of a company official—and was certainly a state-of-the-art piece of steam technology when built in 1889.

34

Manitou & Pikes Peak Railway No. 6

Rack-and-adhesion locomotives were always a technological wonder to all who beheld them in action. Designed to climb incredibly steep grades, usually for very short distances, they could make an adhesion-geared engine, such as a Shay, look helpless. While used on mountain industrial lines in many parts of the world, they occasionally even worked short steep sections of main-line track. They are best known in America, however, for two tourist railroads: the Mount Washington Cog Railway in New Hampshire (which is still in steam) and the Manitou & Pikes Peak Railway in Colorado, which, though long dieselized, has restored a steam engine to active service. A typical M. & P.P. steamer, with its forward-tilted boiler and adhesion wheels as well as a gearing system (hidden by the heavy plate frame) that engaged a rack of toothlike protrusions between the rails, this Vauclain compound (vintage ca. 1880) could tackle 25 percent grades.

35

Sinnemahoning Valley Railroad No. 3

Sometimes a locomotive emerged from the erecting shop looking to all the world as though both the designers and builders had done their work in a state of total inebriation! Such an example was 0–6–6–0T no. 3, named *Edward T. Johnson*, of the Sinnemahoning Valley Railroad in Pennsylvania. Built when Baldwin was aggressively marketing the moderately successful concept of compounding developed by its senior engineer, Samuel Vauclain, this 1891 specimen appears to be one of the earlier four-cylinder locomotives, but it actually possessed no fewer than eight! The high- and low-pressure cylinders were built into the same casting (the former being the smaller one on the bottom) and drove two pistons attached to each crosshead. Although at first appearance, there seems to be a separate tender,

there is not, since boiler and tender both ride on the same rigid frame, with additional water being carried in panion tanks along either side of the boiler. The true oddity, however, is that it looks as though the shop forces had assembled the boiler, cab and tender units and then rolled the frame, wheels, cylinders and machinery backward beneath the orthodox-appearing upper portion! Vauclain's compounds were all the vogue among many railway motive-power departments at the end of the nineteenth century, but most of them were rebuilt as conventional locomotives within less than a decade of delivery from Baldwin, leading to speculation that Vauclain's system of steam distribution was perhaps the most prolific of all failed locomotive designs.

The Vauclain compound design was unusually powerful and efficient in certain uses, as well as compact, so it was most popular for use on diminutive urban rapid-transit locomotives. Chicago's South Side Rapid Transit line required donkey engines that could accelerate quickly and stop short every few blocks. With its high-pressure cylinders below exhausting directly into the low-pressure ones above, engines such as 0–4–4T no. 1 were ideally suited for this demanding service. With a clear view in all directions from the ample cab and a four-wheel truck beneath, these locomotives ran equally well forward or backward. Once technology allowed for the electrification of downtown rapid-transit lines, these little locos were retired by the hundreds almost overnight, just after the turn of the century.

36

South Side Rapid
Transit No. 1

A well-proportioned locomotive-and-tender set, Greenfield & Northern 4-4-0 no. 4, *Hattie J.*, built by Baldwin in 1893, was equipped with Westinghouse airbrakes, which were coming into general use at the time. Prior to the invention of the airbrake, controlling a train was a nerve-wracking exercise that frequently resulted in wrecks, and the hapless brakeman's job was as dangerous as the coal miner's. Originally, the only way to slow a locomotive was to throw the valve gear into reverse. Even when engines were fitted with steam brakes, there was no means of rapidly halting the cars behind. When the engineer whistled "down brakes," the crewmen would clamber up ladders and run along catwalks atop wildly swaying boxcars. This was difficult enough in clear, dry weather, but during heavy rain and wind—or, worse, in ice storms or blizzards—the task was filled with peril as the brakemen scampered from car to car to tighten the handbrakes, controlled by wheels (as they still are). Falling between the cars or being decapitated by an unnoticed low bridge or wire were occurrences all too frequent. When the engineer could apply brakes to the entire train almost at once by manipulating just two valve handles, the number of brakemen required on each train was greatly reduced, as were the rates of mortality and severe injury.

37
—————
Greenfield &
Northern Railroad
No. 4

38

Lehigh Valley Railroad No. 708

The Lehigh Valley was so involved in coal traffic that it proudly called itself "The Route of the Black Diamond"; in the glory days of rail travel, its premier passenger train also was named after the carbon commodity that had powered the Industrial Revolution and literally and figuratively put coal haulers such as the L.V. "in the black." To prevent some of that black from wafting down on the countryside, as well as on the celluloid collars and bonnets of their passengers, most Northeastern roads (with the notable exception of the two largest, the New York Central and the Pennsylvania) opted for the wide-firebox camelback engine. Especially designed to burn much cleaner anthracite coal, the center-cab locomotives, such as Lehigh Valley 4–6–0 no. 708 of the 1890s, were as interesting in appearance as they were in concept. To improve the engineer's visibility, the cab was relocated astride the boiler, separating the fireman at the rear. Although often awkward in appearance, camelbacks could be handsome; certainly no. 708 was an engine of pleasing proportions.

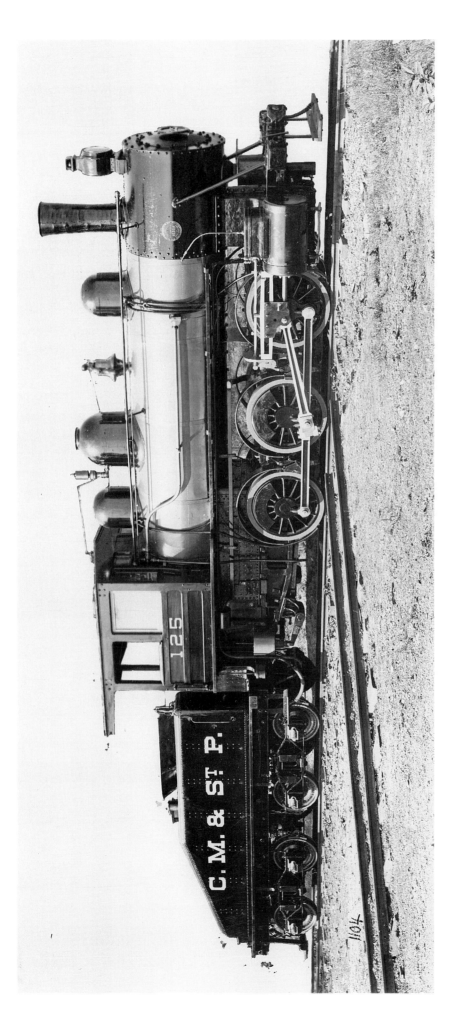

39

Chicago, Milwaukee & St. Paul Railway No. 125

Switch engines were referred to as "yard goats" in the colorful slang of American railroaders, because they were always butting cars around as they made up and disassembled main-line trains. The salient characteristic of the American switcher was the absence of pilot or trailing wheels; all of the shunter's weight was carried on its driving wheels, greatly increasing its power. Another distinguishing feature of many "goats" was the slope-back tender, which enabled the engineer to see the brakemen who coupled and uncoupled cars behind. Chicago, Milwaukee & St. Paul no. 125, an 1898 graduate of Baldwin's Eddystone Works, was an archetypal switcher of her era, simple, rugged and unadorned, not at all bestowed with the elegance of the passenger engines that were her contemporaries. The builder—perhaps at the request of the purchaser—had made but one concession to frivolity; the addition of small fenders ("splashers" in the British lexicon) above each wheel.

40

Pittsburgh, Cincinnati, Chicago & St. Louis Railroad No. 2

The efforts of railroads to hold down the costs of operating passenger service on lightly patronized branch lines resulted in the concept of combining the motive power and the revenue (passenger, mail, baggage, even l.c.l. [less-than-carload] freight) compartments in a single unit. Early on, this was accomplished by enclosing a tiny steam locomotive in the head end of a large wooden car. The concept was updated in the 1920s using gasoline and, later, diesel power, culminating in the renowned Rail Diesel Car (RDC) of the Budd Company in the 1950s. Perhaps the epitome of the pioneering steam cars, Pittsburgh, Cincinnati, Chicago & St. Louis no. 2, built at the zenith of the coach manufacturer's art in 1898, looked at first glance much like a typical handsome combination car of the time, with its gold

striping and serif lettering. The lead truck, however, was actually a 2–4–0 steam locomotive powered by Vauclain compound cylinders, the boiler hidden in the lead compartment and the exhaust carried through a vent above the roof, which dispersed it at the rear of the car, reducing annoyance to passengers. Right aft of the engine compartment was a small baggage section and, beyond that, seating for about forty passengers. Capable of speeds up to sixty miles per hour (faster in cars with taller driving wheels), the power plants of these cars were often strong enough to allow the coupling of one or even a pair of trailing cars to make up a train capable of carrying up to 160 passengers, or 100 passengers and a mail or express car.

41
Erie Railroad
No. 512

Among camelbacks, as well as standard locomotives, the 4–4–2, or "Atlantic" type (named for the Atlantic Coast Line, which had originated it in 1895), was considered the ultimate in passenger power. While even so quintessential a passenger design as the 4–6–2 (the "Pacific" type) was sometimes used in freight service, the Atlantic type was almost never called for any duties but fast limiteds. Erie no. 512 was a splendid example of the camelback Atlantic used by numerous railroads in the Northeastern United States. Built by Baldwin in 1899, she was a high-drivered four-cylinder Vauclain compound designed for speeds exceeding a hundred miles per hour. Even when the 4–4–2 was supplanted by heavier, more powerful designs, surviving examples ran out their active years in fast commuter service. It was just because the Atlantics were poorly adapted for any other use that most went to scrap long before their time and so few (just seven in all of North America) were preserved, just one of which is a camelback.

42
Seaboard Air Line
Railway No. 606

The ubiquitous 4–4–0 had grown considerably in size, weight and power by 1900, the year that Baldwin created the sleek but chunky no. 606 for the Seaboard Air Line subsidiary Florida & West India Short Line. Typical main-line passenger power of that time, the American type still handled the great majority of express trains, even as the much larger 4–4–2 Atlantics were powering heavier consists and the advent of the 4–6–2 Pacific—which became the most popular passenger locomotive worldwide in the twentieth century—was but a few years in the future. High-driving-wheel 4–4–0s were swift, but not too powerful, with engines such as no. 606 capable of handling about six wooden Pullmans at speeds of seventy to ninety miles per hour. The 4–4–2s moved ten similar cars at those speeds, while their successor 4–6–2s would ultimately power a dozen much heavier steel cars at over a hundred m.p.h.

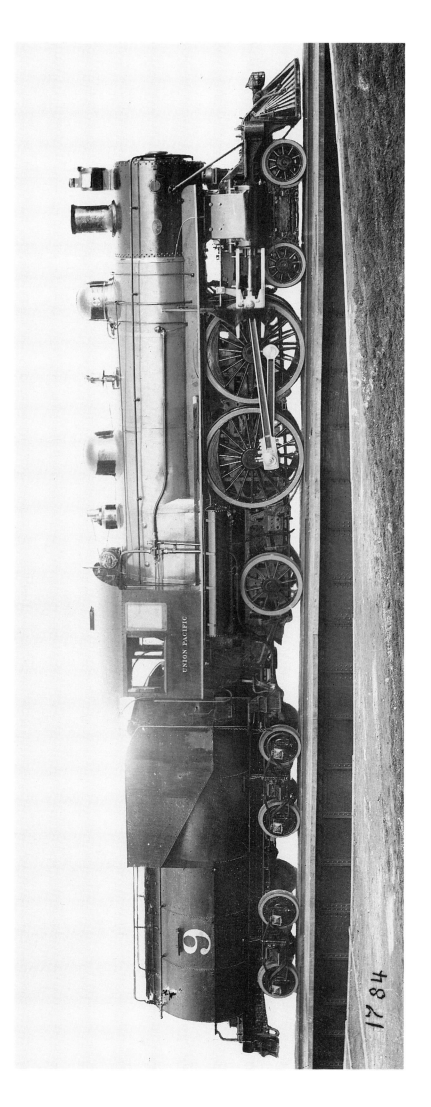

43

Union Pacific Railroad No. 9

By 1900, the sleek 4–4–2 Atlantic type had become the state-of-the-art hauler of express trains. Although its dominance was short-lived (its successor, the 4–6–2, was well established by 1905 and virtually no Atlantics were built after 1914), some 4–4–2s survived in regular service on U.S. main lines into the mid-1950s, and the Atlantic will always be regarded as the classic example of the fastest of all steam-locomotive designs. With driving wheels normally spanning 80–86 inches and an ample-capacity firebox carried over the frame, Atlantics were renowned for running in excess of a hundred miles per hour at the head of light trains (five to eight cars weighing less than 500 tons). (Pacifics, however, could almost equal their speed with 800-ton loads.) Union Pacific no. 9 was a typical aesthetically pleasing 4–4–2, whose bulky tender, unfortunately, looked more as if it belonged behind a plodding branch-line 2–8–0.

When steam locomotives first brought great disturbances to the tranquil countryside, a chorus of complaints and denunciations arose from indignant citizens, particularly carriage and wagon owners whose horses were spooked by the noise, smoke and oscillating machinery of the frightening contraptions. Thereafter the citizenry, often backed by legal authorities, sought to nullify the adverse effects of the engines by getting their operators to resort to various means of disguising their inherently noxious features, such as was done with street-railway locomotives by enclosing them in car bodies, as shown previously in this volume. The purpose of the hinged steel panels that covered the entire power mechanism of this little 0–4–0T, built by Baldwin for the W. I. Company in October 1904, is lost in history, but it probably was more of a safety measure for workers who may have labored in tight-clearance areas, such as tunnels or mine shafts, rather than the calming of animals.

44
W. I. Company
No. 16

45

Southern Pacific
Railway No. 3048

Built by Baldwin in the winter of 1905–06, Southern Pacific 4–4–2 no. 3048 was a typical medium-size high-wheel Atlantic with an electric headlight—an unusually advanced feature for that date. With her 81-inch driving wheels, the 3048 could propel an Espee premier train of eight wood or six steel passenger cars at sustained speeds of over a hundred miles per hour. Of only seven 4–4–2s surviving in the United States, one, no. 3025, is a twin sister of this locomotive, having been built by the American Locomotive Company's Schenectady Works in August 1904. The fastest recorded speed of a steam locomotive was attained by a Pennsylvania Railroad E-2-class Atlantic in 1905, which reached a sustained speed of 127.1 m.p.h. The engine was eventually scrapped, but the Pennsy took a similar machine and renumbered it 7002 (that of the record holder) years later, then displayed it as the authentic locomotive! The "7002" (actually no. 8063, a modernized E-7s) is now displayed at the State Railroad Museum of Pennsylvania at Strasburg, after having operated extensively in the 1980s. Incredibly, the Museum, in other respects a fine institution interested in historical accuracy, refuses to rectify the blatant hoax.

Great Northern Railway No. 1800

The earliest compound, articulated Mallets were modest in size, those being purchased by Class One railroads having two sets of driving gear with six wheels each. Road engines had a pair of nonpowered wheels fore and aft, creating the very popular 2–6–6–2, or Mallet, arrangement, which was destined to become the final type to be built for domestic use by Baldwin (for the Chesapeake & Ohio in 1949) and the last to be built as an articulated for export (to Brazil in 1950). In the twentieth century, only the Pennsylvania and the Great Northern made extensive use of the square Belpaire firebox; 2–6–6–2 no. 1800, built by Baldwin in 1906, was a hallmark G.N. locomotive. In compounding, the smaller, high-pressure cylinders invariably drove the rear engine, while the much larger low-pressure set powered the lead engine. Because this was an articulated locomotive, the front engine was held to the rigid frame with a large pin to allow it to swivel freely, and the lubricating lines to the low-pressure cylinders were coiled up to the boiler, thus allowing flexibility of movement. Round off the Belpaire, add piston-valve cylinders and an electrical lighting system and there is little technological difference between Great Northern no. 1800 and the 2–6–6–2s sent to Brazil 44 years later. While steam-locomotive technology advanced at a brisk pace right up through World War II, certain wheel arrangements, like the 2–6–6–2, seemed not to be as adaptable to massive improvements as others.

Throughout the first century of the steam locomotive, there were occasional designs that were incredible in concept and even bizarre in appearance. Few could surpass the dinky narrow-gauge 0–4–0T steam car built for the Ferrocarril de Guantánamo (Guantánamo Railroad), Cuba, by Baldwin in 1906. The entire outer shell of the diminutive vertical-boiler engine consisted of a standard tender tank—somewhat modified in front and back for crew access. With most tenderless tank engines, it is still apparent which end is the front and which is the rear. Not so with this one. With the roof running the entire length and oil headlights on each end, there is no telling where the front is! The only clue—apart from the shape of the tender-turned-locomotive—lies in the photograph itself, since builder shots were made from the front. In railroad terminology a "tender locomotive" refers to an engine with a tender (as opposed to a tank engine); this little monstrosity gives a totally unintended new meaning to the term!

47
───────
Ferrocarril de Guantánamo

48

Dai Nippon Seito Kwaisha, Ltd., No. 1

Dinky little narrow-gauge 0–4–0 tank engines were built by locomotive manufacturers in the major industrial nations and exported to virtually every colony and undeveloped country for use on plantations, in mines and in industries. In the Far East, Japan was rapidly industrializing by 1900; indeed it managed to defeat Imperial Russia decisively in a brief but far-reaching conflict just a few years later. Despite its progress, however, Japan still found it expeditious, well into the twentieth century, to import some steam locomotives. One of them was a delightful, surprisingly well-proportioned little saddletanker for Dai Nippon Seito Kwaisha, Ltd., turned out by Baldwin subsidiary Burnham, Williams & Co. in April 1907. With an outrageously tall diamond smokestack, the height of which equaled that from the railhead to the top of its boiler, no. 1 also sported a steam dome and sandbox worthy of a standard-gauge engine. Except for the large cab (the engineers even of narrow-gauge locomotives required standard-gauge cabs!), this little weed-cutter of an engine is an exceptionally pretty work mule.

Among the rolling stock exported by American locomotive builders were a few steam-powered railcars, such as the one erected by Baldwin as no. 1 for the South Manchurian Railway in China in 1907. The angle of this photograph, with the windows of the boiler compartment purposely opened to reveal the power plant, illustrates how thoroughly the little locomotive was integrated with the car body. The armrests indicate that the engineer could operate the machine from either the first or second windows (perhaps using one for running forward and the other for reverse). The passenger compartment could seat only about 24, but the locomotive, although small, generated enough power to enable the coupling of one or perhaps two additional cars for added capacity. With sweeping cowcatchers at both ends, no. 1 could run equally well in either direction. Interestingly, the logo of the China Railways under the Communist regime consists of a circle enclosing an end view of a track rail, very similar to the circular "M" and rail of the early-1900s South Manchurian Railway.

49
_____

South Manchurian Railway No. 1

50

Lehigh & Hudson River Railway No. 64

The Lehigh & Hudson River Railway was a noteworthy employer of camelbacks, a typical example being no. 64, erected by Baldwin in 1907. This was a transition locomotive, bridging the gap between the cruder technology of the nineteenth century and the more sophisticated engine improvements of the early 1900s. While the stack and domes, as well as the cab and wheel counterweights, were of 1880s vintage, the electric headlight and generator, double airpumps and piston-valve cylinders were very much twentieth-century devices. With ample tender, a locomotive of this design would remain basically unimproved over a service life of thirty to forty years, while one built less than ten years earlier would probably have been extensively rebuilt—including a larger boiler—by 1920.

51
Atchison, Topeka &
Santa Fe Railway
No. 1301

In modern times, the huge two-cylinder 4–8–4s and 2–10–4s were so powerful that the Atchison, Topeka & Santa Fe didn't even bother with articulated types so favored by competitors Southern Pacific and Union Pacific; A.T. & S.F. just ordered some of the largest and heaviest standard engines ever built! Back before the First World War, however, Santa Fe had a wild fling with compound articulateds, including massive 2–10–10–2s and—perhaps most noteworthy—a 4–4–6–2 design that was to be the only four-cylinder two-engine passenger locomotive until the Pennsylvania's S-1 6–4–4–6 of 1939 and T-1 4–4–4–4 of 1942. In 1909, A.T. & S.F. combined the two most popular passenger designs of the time—the 4–4–2 and the 4–6–2—into its long-boilered 4–4–6–2, seen here. Powerful and speedy, it could pull a heavy train, but the inadequate firebox could not deliver the sustained steaming required by the two high-pressure and two low-pressure cylinders. During World War I, the 2–10–10–2s were rebuilt into 2–10–2s and the unorthodox passenger power didn't last much longer. No. 1301's tender was of special interest: incredibly large for its time, it rode on six-wheel passenger-car trucks, its size giving no. 1301 the fuel and water range of a Pacific with a typical tender.

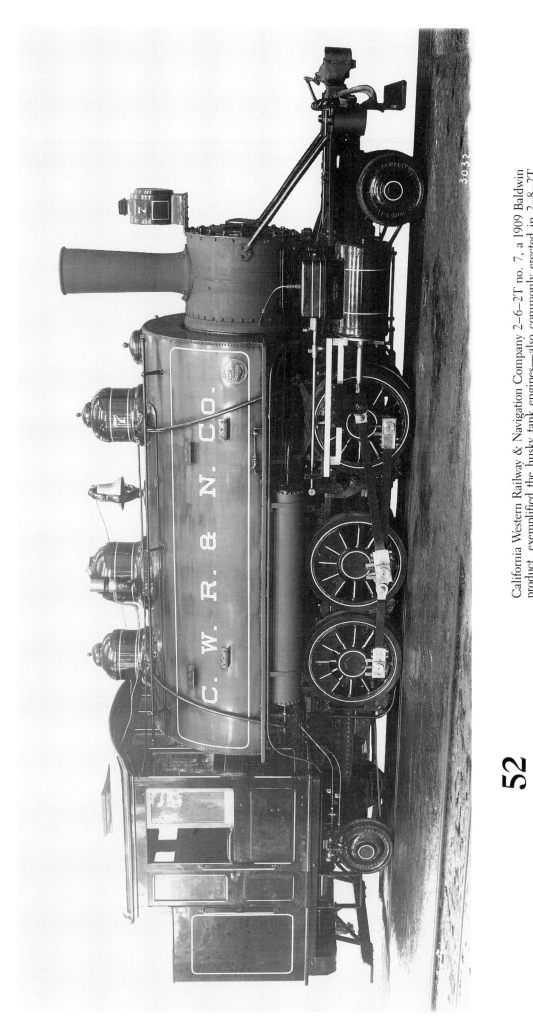

52

California Western Railway & Navigation Company No. 7

California Western Railway & Navigation Company 2–6–2T no. 7, a 1909 Baldwin product, exemplified the husky tank engines—also commonly erected in 2–8–2T configuration—that were to ply the better-graded logging lines of the Pacific Northwest right up to the end of steam in the early 1960s. Usually—but not always—the trailing truck's function was to carry the weight of the fuel bunker behind the cab, in this case implying that, had this been a tender engine, it would have been a 2–6–0. Such was not the case with no. 7 and similar designs, for the firebox, located behind the rear driving axle, required the trailing wheels. Had the bunker been much larger, however, an additional trailing axle would have been necessary on account of axle loading on light track and bridges. Then this would have become a 2–6–4T, a rare design in America, but more popular in Europe and the Far East.

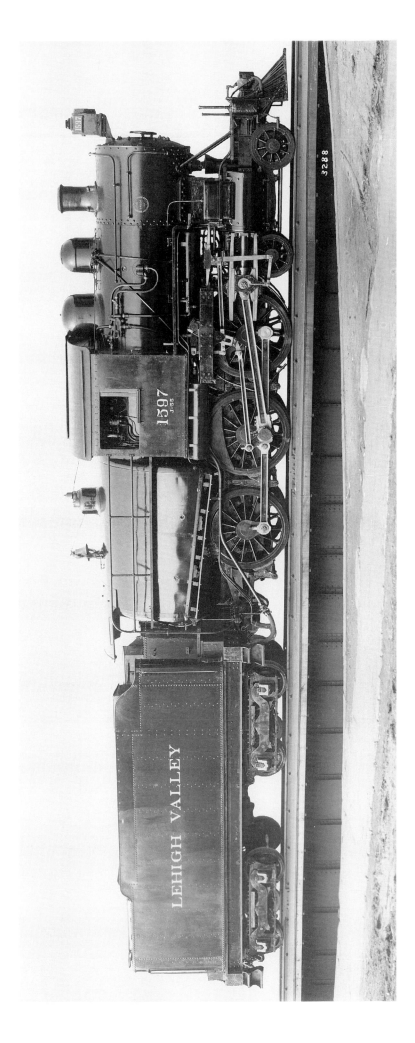

53
Lehigh Valley
Railroad No. 1597

One of the world's most popular wheel arrangements was the 4–6–0, built in the United States between the 1860s and the 1920s, and overseas at even later dates. The ten-wheeler was also probably the most common of all camelback types, with virtually every company that rostered the center-cab engines fielding at least one class of them. In fact, the last camelbacks in regular service were Central Railroad of New Jersey 4–6–0s, which ran until 1954. Those of the Lehigh Valley, such as no. 1597, built in 1910, were well proportioned and, like most ten-wheelers with driving wheels in the 67- to 75-inch range, were well suited for both medium freight and heavy passenger duties, hence their popularity. Although fascinating in form, camelbacks were inherently dangerous creatures, since the engineer and fireman were separated by the firebox and unable to communicate. Normally, the crewmen would call out signal aspects and other potential problems to each other for verification; this was an impossibility with camelbacks. If the engineer suffered a heart

attack or stroke, the fireman might not realize it until the train sped through the next station stop at seventy miles per hour! At high speed a driving or connecting rod could break and spin upward; if it crashed through the deck of a center-cab engine, the engineer could be sliced in half. At a time when management cared little about the basic comfort of the workers, a camelback was especially vexatious, allowing just two feet of space between the boiler and the cab wall and leaving the fireman to shovel coal on a windswept, exposed and undulating platform. Of these locomotives it was often said that "in the summer the engineer roasted and in the winter the fireman froze." The last batch was built for the Jersey Central in 1918. After ascertaining that no railroad had intentions of purchasing any additional ones, the Federal government outlawed them—albeit with a "grandfather clause" that allowed the thousand or more then in existence to run out their normal service lives.

By 1910, the boilers of even modest-size steam locomotives had reached robust dimensions and, with the wide Wootten firebox required to burn anthracite coal efficiently, a sustained level of steaming was attainable. Lehigh & New England 2–8–0 no. 32, a Baldwin graduate of 1911, was a camelback of large boiler circumference with cylinders to match. This three-quarter view taken from the front illustrates how cramped and inhospitable the narrow engineer's cab was and why during the heat of summer a sootblackened, sweat-soaked engineer, wearing just trousers and a thin undershirt, could often be seen sitting on the armrest, with just his legs inside the hot cab while performing switching moves. Once on the road at speed, with the front door open, he was cooled by breezes, somewhat alleviating the discomfort. Since many of Baldwin's builder photos were shot on the turntable outside the erecting hall, by this time some official had gotten the sensible idea of lettering the name of the company on the outside timber of the catwalk.

54

Lehigh & New England Railroad No. 32

55

Nashville, Chattanooga & St. Louis Railroad No. 290

The 4–6–2 Pacific type (so named because the first one was built for the Missouri Pacific in 1903) had been growing in popularity for nearly a decade when an unremarkable series of low-drivered examples was built by Baldwin for the Nashville, Chattanooga & St. Louis in 1912. Although equipped with such modern accessories as power reverse and electric lighting, no. 290 actually more closely resembled a short-line or export locomotive, rather than a main-line flyer, or even the N.C. & St. L. Pacifics built just a few years later. The 4–6–2 was about to come to the forefront as the premier passenger-hauler—not only in the United States, but around the world—and no. 290 represented but a step in the evolutionary progression toward a truly heavy-duty yet speedy all-purpose express locomotive.

Pennsylvania
Railroad No. 5400

The year 1914 saw the opening of the Panama Canal, the beginning of World War I and the development of the Pennsylvania Railroad's K-4s Pacific locomotive. With its mammoth boiler, eighty-inch driving wheels and the ability to hold down demanding passenger schedules over the next 43 years without any major design changes, the K-4s was destined to become one of history's truly great locomotives. Compared to the relatively anemic Nashville, Chattanooga & St. Louis 4–6–2 of just two years previously, the buxom-boilered K-4s proved to be a landmark engine, even able to compete successfully with archrival New York Central's superb 4–6–4 design of 1927, the same year that the final order of K-4s's locomotives was placed. Of the 425 K-4s's built, 75 were constructed by Baldwin, the initial one being no. 5400. Although thirteen years younger than the prototype, virtually the only differences were cosmetic—electric headlight, steel pilot, larger tender. From the outset, the Pennsy's Altoona works had designed a true thoroughbred, worthy of the acclaim it received.

57

Louisiana State Penitentiary "Jack"

Many odd little switch engines were built for public and private institutions as on-grounds shunters. Industrial switchers were quite common; they were utilized by factories, mines, large agricultural concerns, military bases, steel mills and shipyards to move freight cars around and assemble blocks of cars to be picked up by the connecting common-carrier railroads. Institutions, such as large state mental hospitals, prisons and warehouse complexes, often maintained a solitary small steam locomotive to do light on-premises shifting of cars. Tank engines were popular for this work, since they operated within a short radius of their servicing facilities and did not require a large fuel and water capacity. Other complexes used tender locomotives either out of habit, or because such an engine could be acquired cheaply—most often secondhand from a shortline or even a major railway. The small 0–6–0 named *Jack* had no number when it was built

by Lima in 1913 for the Board of Control State Penitentiary of Louisiana. The affable little grunger was pleasing in appearance, with a slender tall stack, ample domes and cab, and a traditional slope-back tender. Other than in builder portraits such as this, the locomotives in this service were rarely photographed. Visitors to state hospitals or prisons had on their minds concerns other than train photography, and railway historians simply overlooked the small, sometimes inaccessible institutional locomotives in favor of the big show of nearby main-line engines thundering down the high iron. That was unfortunate, for a picture of the little *Jack* backing a pair of coal hoppers to the prison power station or leaving the interchange track with a reefer load of beef bound for the siding alongside the kitchen would have been of more than passing fascination.

Croft Lumber Company No. 4

While the Shay was by far the most popular and common of the geared adhesion locomotives, there were two other successful designs, the Climax and the Heisler, both of which were powered by a shaft beneath the center of the locomotive, rather than on the outside. The Heisler had two cylinders mounted in a "V" arrangement (similar to that of an internal-combustion engine), which powered a shaft leading to the inside axle of each truck. A ratchet gear powered the axles and regular connecting rods ran from the outside of the wheels on those axles to the outer wheels on each truck. Croft Lumber Company no. 4, built by Baldwin in 1913, was similar to the Climax. It had its cylinders mounted much like those on a conventional rod-driven engine, but the power was transmitted via a crosswise shaft that was geared to the lengthwise shaft and geared to all axles. The Climax was built by

the Climax Manufacturing Company of Corry, Pennsylvania; it is a mystery how Baldwin got to erect this example. Either it was done on license from the patent holder or the Baldwin plans were just sufficiently at variance with the original to avoid a patent infringement. This locomotive is also unusual in that it has three trucks; virtually all Climaxes were of the smaller two-truck variety. Although eclipsed by the Shay, both the Climax and the Heisler were used extensively in the same types of logging and industrial situations, and an appreciable number of each have been preserved in North America. Recently, an exquisite example of a narrow-gauge Corry-built Climax was completely restored. It now runs on the renowned museum line, the Puffing Billy Railway, in Australia.

Nevada–
California–Oregon
Railway No. 14

Although Nevada–California–Oregon sounds impressive as a railroad corporate name, it was but a three-foot-gauge shortline little remarked in the annals of railway history. The 2–8–0 no. 14, turned out by Baldwin in 1914, was serviced by a round-top tender of the type long associated with the Southern Pacific's famed Owens Valley Line in eastern California, a desolate narrow-gauge branch destined to gain fame when it remained in steam until the mid-1950s. Although even at this late date virtually all locomotives (including no. 14) still sported antiquated kerosene headlights, some major railroads were already using electricity, hence the steam turbo-generator in the left foreground, destined no doubt for a Pacific- or Mountain-type express passenger engine of a major company.

60
Erie Railroad No. 2603

The early twentieth century saw an enormous and rapid increase in the sheer dimensions of the American steam locomotive. In 1900, the Pittsburgh Locomotive Works erected what was then the world's heaviest and most powerful locomotive, a 2–8–0, for the Pittsburgh, Bessemer & Lake Erie Railroad. Just fourteen years later, Baldwin built the engine seen here, no. 2603, named *Matt H. Shay*, for the Erie, a gargantuan 2–8–8–8–2T Triplex, with six cylinders powering 24 driving wheels, compared to the earlier engine's two cylinders and eight drivers! The Erie monster did not live up to expectations and was never duplicated, for reasons that should have been obvious to the designers. First, any firebox that was to provide sustained steaming for *six cylinders* working a five-thousand-ton coal train upgrade, as *Matt* was expected to do, would have had to be much larger than anything contemplated in 1914. Secondly, since the third engine of the set supported the tender, two major problems occurred. The wheels

and machinery took up so much room that the coal and water capacity was severely restricted, necessitating constant stops for replenishing. There was also the problem of weight. The tractive effort of a locomotive (determining its power) is directly related to the weight on its driving wheels. In the Triplex, the rear set lost much of its effectiveness and began to slip as the levels of water and coal were reduced, since this gradually removed much of the weight needed to keep the driving wheels working properly. An even larger 2–8–8–8–4T was tried, but it too was not a success. Even with the development of huge fireboxes in the late 1920s, the Triplex concept was never resurrected, the final development of gargantuan steam locomotives being of the four-cylinder simple variety (with all cylinders operating at high pressure) in 2–8–8–4, 2–6–6–4, 4–6–6–4, 4–8–8–4 and 2–6–6–6 wheel arrangements.

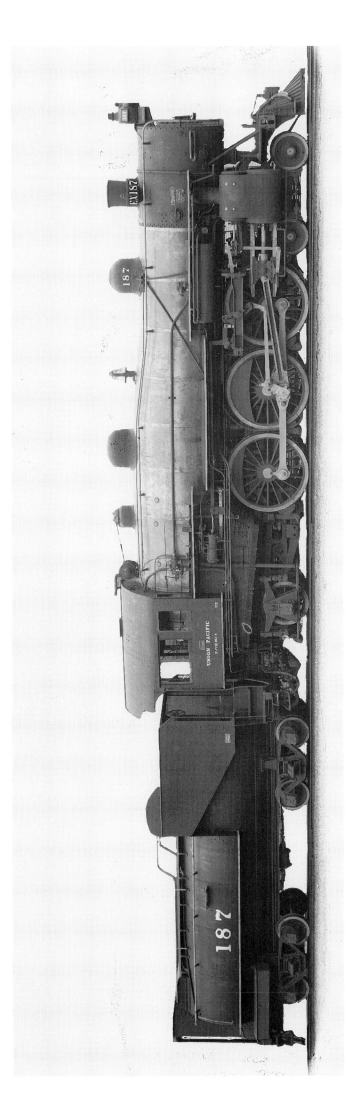

61
Union Pacific Railroad No. 187

By 1914, the 4–6–2 had greatly matured in size and performance. From this point it changed little over the next 34 years, when the final American examples of the type were built by the Reading railroad in 1948. Certainly, the twenty Pacifics built for the Union Pacific in 1914, like no. 187, and five additional ones erected for its subsidiary, the Oregon Short Line, were of ample proportions and, riding on 77-inch driving wheels, could handle heavy passenger trains at timetable speeds. Even when superseded by 4–8–2s in the 1920s and 4–8–4s in the 1930s, 4–6–2s of the World War I era soldiered on until the end of the steam era, hauling secondary passenger and commuter trains as well as handling light freight chores.

62

Great Northern Railway No. 1755

The 4–8–2, or "Mountain," type was a dual-service wheel arrangement, equally at home pulling fast freights or heavy passenger trains. While some were designed specifically for freight and others for passenger duties, most could handle both; a lot depended on their driving-wheel diameter. In many instances, a railroad had both missions in mind when designing an engine. The Great Northern Railway's 4–8–2 of 1914, with its relatively low 62-inch driving wheels, was a freight engine that never aspired to moving varnish. No. 1755 was one of ten built in the series; with its Belpaire firebox it closely resembled a Pennsylvania Railroad locomotive. A comparison of no. 1755 with the P.R.R. M-1, conceived just nine years later, shows how rapidly the 4–8–2 grew in size, power, mission and concept in less than a decade.

63
Pennsylvania Railroad No. 9710

The Pennsylvania Railroad proudly advertised that it was "the Standard Railroad of the World," and as such many of its practices—and locomotive designs—were uniform and predictable. In the mid-1910s the Pennsy ordered hundreds of nearly identical H-9s and H-10s Consolidation-type freight engines, many of which were to survive until the end of steam, more than forty years later. Although many of the P.R.R. locomotives were not only designed but built in the company's sprawling Juniata Shops in the heart of Altoona, Pennsylvania, it often turned to the commercial builders when it required large numbers of locomotives in a hurry. Such was the case with the big 2–8–0s, and all three major builders, as well as the Penn itself, churned them out. No. 9710, erected by Baldwin's Eddystone Works in 1915, was a typical member of the H-10s clan, her centered headlight declaring that she was soon to be assigned to Lines West (of Pittsburgh), since Eastern region engines' headlights were always mounted high on the smokebox. So standardized was Pennsy's policy that management required that Baldwin substitute for its usual round builder's plate one identical with the oval-shaped one of the Juniata Shops!

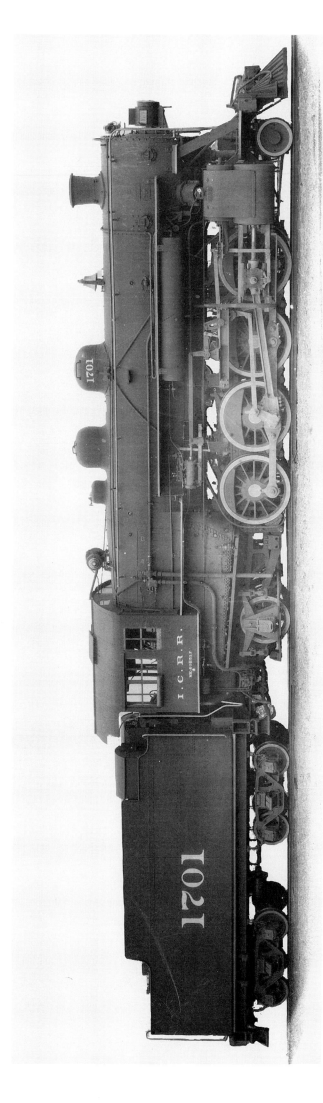

Illinois Central
Railroad No. 1701

The Illinois Central, which began extending its main line south from the frontier village of Chicago in the 1840s, was to become the chief transport rival to Mississippi riverboat operators as well as the dominant north–south railroad in the United States. Priding itself early on as being the "Main Line of Mid-America," the I.C. long lived up to its reputation by highballing freight and luxury passenger trains down to New Orleans. It also rode into the folklore of the nation when, on April 30, 1900, one of its most daring and reputable young engineers—named John Luther "Casey" Jones—made his legendary "trip to the promised land." Casey (so nicknamed because he was a native of Cayce, Kentucky) was piloting one of the largest engines on the Illinois Central roster at the time, a 4–6–0. Just fifteen years later, the railroad was investing a vast amount of money in 2–8–2s—the "Mikado" type—which were twice the size and strength of the older ten-wheelers. In one clip, the I.C. gave Lima its first single

fifty-locomotive order when it acquired heavy Mikados nos. 1701–1750 in 1915, shortly before the entry of the United States into the First World War. The 2–8–2 was just what the company needed; by the late 1920s, it stabled hundreds of them. In 1926, the Illinois Central tested Lima's revolutionary A-1 2–8–4 and was so impressed that it ordered fifty copies—and insisted on purchasing the prototype demonstrator as well! The old Mikados lasted until the end of steam in 1960, the I.C. shops in Paducah, Kentucky, having become extremely adept at upgrading and rebuilding older engines, extending their useful life by years. They even built a modest fleet of brand-new 4–8–2s during World War II and kept on modernizing the old "Mikes" right into the 1950s. Other railroad shops were well equipped and had highly motivated craftsmen, but none exceeded the accomplishments of Paducah.

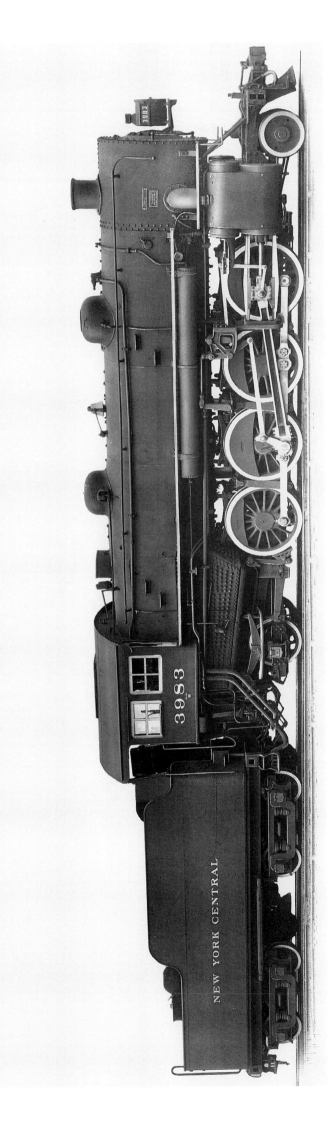

65

New York Central Railroad No. 3983

When it came to fielding an almost universal freight locomotive after 1910, American railroads loved the 2–8–2 and ordered thousands of them over the next two decades and beyond. The New York Central purchased them by the hundreds, right up to the coming of their very successful 4–8–2 types (which were also well suited for heavy fast-passenger duties) and put them to good use all over their far-flung system. No. 3983, erected by Lima in 1916, was a very typical Mikado of its time; the inadequately small tender was later replaced with a larger one that gave the engine greater range between coal and water stops.

Virginian Railway
No. 700

The largest of the Triplex locomotives was also the only one with a 2–8–8–8–4T wheel arrangement, erected for the Virginian Railway by Baldwin in 1916. It was huge and, as if the six cylinders were not enough to starve the boiler and inadequate firebox of steam, a low-speed booster engine was mounted on the four-wheel trailing truck! No. 700 spent her brief life mostly in helper service on the steep grades of western Virginia, where she exerted power that was unprecedented but that could not long be sustained before the steam pressure began dropping.

The idea of carrying around a deadweight tender loaded with fuel and water and weighing as much as 220 tons (three passenger cars or four average freight cars) was anathema to railroad motive-power departments, which were charged with squeezing as much efficiency as possible out of each locomotive design. In the teens, when the Triplex engines (see photos 60 and 66) were being tested, some companies, including the Long Island Rail Road and the Southern Railway, designed orthodox locomotives with an extra set of running gear beneath the tender, theoretically creating what can only be described as an articulated compound tank engine! The L.I.R.R. planned to take an existing 2–8–0 and mount the frame, machinery, wheels and cylinders of a scrapped 0–6–0 beneath the tender, making it a 2–8–0 + 0–6–0T of sorts. After drawing up the blueprints, the L.I.R.R. designers rightly decided not to proceed, since the depletion of coal and water in the tender would so reduce the adhesion of its engine as to render it virtually useless. The Southern, however, decided to prove itself wrong by having Baldwin build a 2–8–2 + 2–8–0T in 1917. With piston-valve cylinders on the locomotive and slide-valve cylinders under the tender, the 4537 went to work, but of course the usual problems of a firebox too small to feed all four cylinders and the poor adhesion of the tender assured eventual failure.

68

Imperial Russian Railways Ye Class No. 541

American locomotives built for export were shipped in the thousands during the first half of the twentieth century, one of the largest early orders being for 875 identical Ye-class 2–10–0s sent to the Imperial Russian Railways during the First World War. No. 541, built by Baldwin in 1917, was a typical example, and even more were built and ordered, but all that had not been shipped after the Communist Revolution of October 1917 were embargoed. Those stranded at American ports were sent back to the manufacturers and converted from the Russian five-foot gauge to standard 4′8½″ gauge and sold by the U.S. government to various American railroads at bargain prices. In a complete change of heart, however, the American authorities agreed, under Lend-Lease in World War II, to send approximately 1,900

nearly identical Russian Decapods (as they had become known to U.S. railwaymen) to the Soviet Union during the 1943–45 period, which was the largest single order of locomotives ever built for export. In total numbers constructed, only the more than 2,100 standard U.S. Army S-160 Consolidations, simultaneously abuilding, added up to more than the Soviet 2–10–0s. The latter ran in Siberia well into the 1970s (when the author managed to photograph them). Some of the World War I Yeˊs, which wound up on such lines as the Erie, the Frisco and the Gainesville Midland, survived into the 1950s. A fair number of the Russian Decapods in the U.S.A. have been preserved, including Frisco no. 1630, which has been restored to operation and runs regularly at the Illinois Railway Museum.

69

Central Railroad of
New Jersey No. 825

Although the Central Railroad of New Jersey is mostly remembered for its large number of camelbacks (it rostered a higher percentage than any other major line), it also boasted large fleets of modern conventional 4–6–2s and 2–8–2s. As built by Baldwin, the 4–6–2 Pacifics were rather basic and plain, but, by the 1930s, various appliances had been added and other changes made that in Cinderella fashion turned some of them into exquisite princesses of the high iron. Pulling such romantically named trains as The Queen of the Valley and The Blue Comet (the latter in blue-and-cream livery with gold striping), these 800-series 4–6–2s ran until the end of C.N.J. steam in the mid-1950s. Like their predecessor camelbacks, they too, had wide Wootten fireboxes, but by this time (1918) it was obvious that a center cab could be optional.

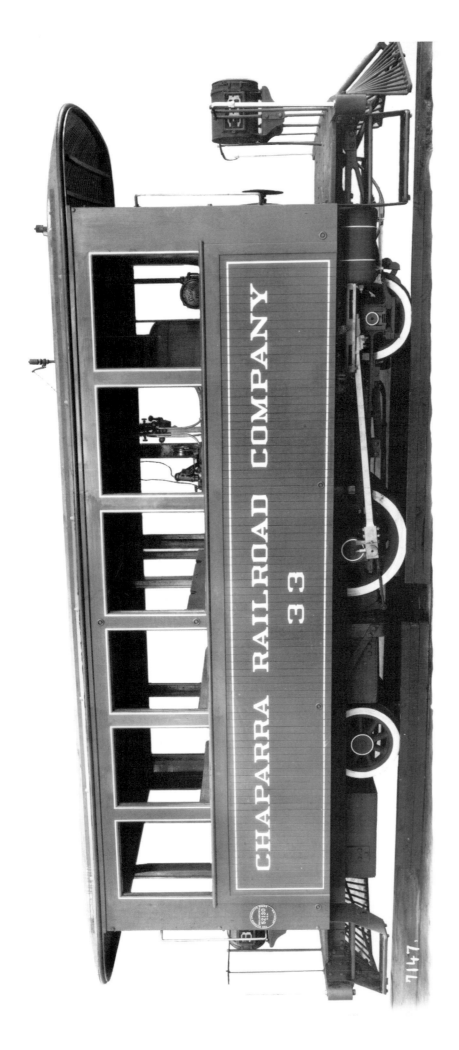

Chaparra Railroad Company No. 33

Unlike the sometimes elegant steam-powered passenger cars and similar inspection engines built for American railways, equipment erected for Latin American lines was frequently very plain in concept and lacking in all but the most basic of amenities. Chaparra Railroad no. 33 had no clerestory roof, plush seats, gilt trim—or windows! Nor was there a barrier between the exposed vertical boiler and the passenger compartment; cinders, dust and rain blew in at will. However, there were electric headlights mounted on each end platform, and riding around in this little steam bus was probably just plain rugged fun and adventure!

71

Kin-Han Railway
No. 351

The 2–6–2 Prairie-type engine was rarely built for main-line service in the United States, but many foreign countries, including Serbia, Hungary, Poland, Russia and others made extensive use of them right up to the end of steam in the 1980s. Although the 2–6–2 type was used by logging roads and other lightweight secondary services until the end of the steam era in America, these engines were essentially of the 2–6–0, or "Mogul," type with the addition of a trailing axle to spread the weight, useful on light, poorly maintained track. No. 351 of the Kin-Han Railway in China, however, was erected by Lima in 1919 as a true Prairie (the firebox was supported by the rear truck) intended for main-line mixed-traffic service. The six-wheel tender with the journals mounted in the frame was of typically European, rather than American, design.

72

Elgin, Joliet &
Eastern Railway
No. 333

At the outset of the First World War, a panicky United States Government lost faith in some of its vital institutions—from American citizens of German ancestry to the vast railroad industry. In the case of the latter, the Federal government foolishly seized the railways and ran them under a colossal, inept bureaucracy called the United States Railway Administration (no relation to the current agency of a similar name), costing billions of dollars in tax funds. Having actually learned a lesson from this stupidity (rare for sure, but government bureaucrats occasionally learn from past mistakes), the feds left the railroads alone during World War II, when they performed extremely well—and *paid* billions in taxes! One good thing did come out of the U.S.R.A. debacle, however: the introduction of standard-design steam locomotives that were parceled out to railroads as they needed them. For nearly a century, the railroads had insisted, for the most part, on designing their own locomotives, a policy that added expenses, discouraged standardization within the industry and unfairly exacerbated the reputation of the steam engine as being expensive to maintain. In fact, when the diesel locomotive was perfected, General Motors wisely initiated a policy that said

in effect to railway motive-power officials: you are not welcome in our drafting and design section. If a railroad wanted to buy other than G.M. standard designs, the cost would be prohibitive. Amazed railroad managements suddenly discovered that the engines run by their competitors, or across the continent, were good enough on their own roads. Of course, the same was possible with steam, as the U.S.R.A. standard designs had proven twenty years earlier. In most cases, a light and a heavy version of each major wheel arrangement was put into production; no. 333 (built around 1918–20), was a heavy 0–8–0, ordered by the government (lettered simply "U.S." on the tender) but assigned to the Elgin, Joliet & Eastern Railway. Most railroads were well pleased with the standard locomotives and even ordered variants of the basic designs for decades to come. Some would not change their thick-headed ways no matter how convincing; the Pennsylvania Railroad, for example, abhorred any engine it did not design itself and that had no Belpaire firebox, so it sold all of its U.S.R.A. locomotives in the early 1920s—almost as soon as the company was returned to its owners by the government.

73

Texas–Mexican Railway No. 1

While the corporate title of the Texas–Mexican Railway aspired to imperial dimensions, its physical extent did not; it boasted a mere 160.1 miles of track—and not a solitary branch line—between the port of Corpus Christi and the Mexican border at Laredo, all within the Lone Star State. Ten-wheeler no. 1, built by Baldwin in 1920, appeared ideally suited for her role: a trim, well-proportioned little road engine designed to haul modest trains over a relatively short railroad. No. 1 was a typical product of the post–World War I era; her demure dimensions and capabilities would have rendered her as practical pulling trainloads of cane at one of the sprawling sugar centrals in Cuba as they did on the unostentatious "Tex-Mex."

74

Missouri, Kansas & Texas Railroad No. 399

The Missouri, Kansas & Texas also ran extensively in Oklahoma but chose not to mention that state in its corporate title, probably because Oklahoma was still Indian territory when the railroad was built. The M.K. & T. (or "Katy," as it was affectionately and, later, officially known) offered a direct fast route between St. Louis and Kansas City in the North and the major cities of Texas in the South. Despite the long distances it traveled across the prairies of the South Central states, the Katy never bought a passenger locomotive larger than the trim Pacifics (no. 399, seen here, and nos. 400–408) of 1920. In fact, its heaviest freight power was the standard World War I United States Railway Administration Mikado of comparable size. The topography of the rights-of-way of the M–K–T (after a bankruptcy reorganization it became the Missouri–Kansas–Texas Railroad) was gener-

ally flat, so it forsook the 4–8–2s and 2–10–4s of its neighbors and never even considered articulated power. In later years, external modifications of the 4–6–2s made them exceedingly handsome racers as they sped The Texas Special, The Bluebonnet, The Katy Flyer and The Katy Limited on their fast schedules. With their 73-inch driving wheels, M–K–T Pacifics were not as fast as some other lines' premier motive power, but they could handle heavier trains and still hit seventy m.p.h. When the name trains were dieselized just after World War II, the 4–6–2s were bumped to secondary locals; then all were scrapped in the 1950s. A modernized 1893 4–4–0, the sole surviving Katy steam locomotive, is currently being rebuilt to operational status by the National Museum of Transport in St. Louis.

Between 1917 and 1923 the New York, Chicago & St. Louis, more commonly known as the Nickel Plate Road, acquired 81 Mikados (including no. 627, seen here, built by Lima in October 1922), which were to be the company's primary freight power until its celebrated 700-series Berkshires began arriving in 1934. When the NKP took over the Lake Erie & Western, it inherited fifteen additional Mikes, one of which, no. 587, was put on display in Indianapolis, and, in 1988, after four years of restoration work by the Indiana Transportation Museum volunteers, was returned to active service hauling excursion trains. Some of the versatile 2–8–2s ran right up until the end of Nickel Plate steam in 1958; others survived until 1965 on the National Railways of Mexico, which purchased 25 of them just after World War II. The Nickel Plate 2–8–2s were very typical of the United States Railway Administration standard World War I designs that were adopted by various Class One railroads in the late teens and twenties. All of these reliable locomotives performed their assigned tasks very well for some forty years, until finally supplanted by diesels.

75

Nickel Plate Road
No. 627

76

Imperial Forestry Railway of Japan

The modest little 0–4–2T purchased from Baldwin in 1923 by the Imperial Forestry Railway of Japan was two-foot gauge or less and probably weighed in at about ten tons, yet it boasted a cab that would have done justice to a standard-gauge Consolidation and was assigned a builder's plate and serial number the same as a five-hundred-ton Mallet. The rounded smokestack, commonly called a "cabbage stack" because of its spherical configuration, was a common spark-arresting device also found on many backwoods engines on American logging roads. In fact, several of the latter survive, including a couple in operating condition.

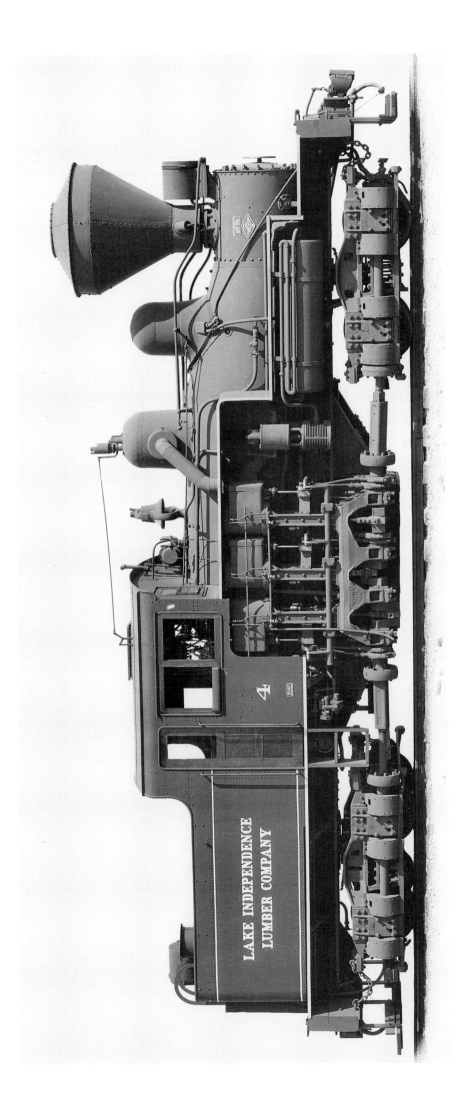

Lake Independence
Lumber Company
No. 4

Because the Shay locomotive was powered only on the right side, it was most appropriately nicknamed "sidewinder" by railroad men. No. 4 of the Lake Independence Lumber Company in Michigan, built in 1923, is a classic example of the most common type of two-truck Shay, hundreds of which were turned out by Lima in the tens and twenties. Although a coal burner, no. 4, in the manner of many logging locos, sported a huge balloon stack right out of the 1850s. Every effort had to be expended to avoid forest fires, and the elaborate netting within the funnel trapped even the smallest sparks. Shay engines were slow—rarely able to exceed twenty m.p.h.—but extremely strong and nimble, as they hauled heavy loads over undulating track on steep grades that would have stalled or derailed a conventional rod-driven locomotive.

78

Grand Trunk
Western Railway
No. 8222

During the 1920s, Lima built scores of chunky 0–8–0 switchers for Grand Trunk Western, a United States subsidiary of Canadian National Railways. Most of them worked on for thirty years and longer, assembling and disassembling the heavy freight trains that supplied the automobile factories of Michigan and the industries of Chicago and Detroit and moved the grain of the Midwest and Canada. Then, in the late 1950s, they went to the scrap yards to be cut up and forgotten. Many of them wound up at the large electric-process mill of the Northwestern Steel & Wire Company, in Sterling, Illinois, where, in a weird and poetic turn of events, sixteen were withheld from scrapping, to be used as switchers by the company. Some of them survived in active service for over twenty years before they were retired in 1980 as the last industrial steam locomotives in the U.S.A. Because of their post-steam-era service at Northwestern, these G.T.W. eight-wheel shunters became quite famous, attracting many railroad photographers, and four were ultimately preserved.

79
Long Island Rail
Road No. 268

Between 1916 and 1924, the Long Island Rail Road, more commonly associated with passenger operations, especially multiple-unit electric trains, had such an increase in its freight business that it ordered four batches of large 0–8–0 switchers from three different American Locomotive Company plants, totaling nineteen engines. Unusually handsome for humble shunters, these C-51sa types, with their long-bunkered slope-back tenders, spent their service lives almost entirely within the Brooklyn and Queens boroughs of New York City, only occasionally working into Nassau County. And their service lives were shorter than might have been expected. Many railroads dieselized their main-line operations first, leaving yard engines in steam, but the L.I.R.R. did just the opposite; since the big shifters were a source of pollution in heavily populated urban areas, virtually all were out of service by 1950, when only half of the railroad's operations in nonelectrified areas was dieselized. As turned out by the Richmond Works in Virginia in 1924, no. 268, like her previous sisters, mounted an odd hood above the front of the tender, an accessory used on some camelbacks in America in the 1880s but in the twentieth century more apt to be found on British-built locomotives in the tropical climes of such places as India, Burma and South America. (*Ron Ziel Collection.*)

80

Maryland and Pennsylvania Railroad No. 43

The Maryland and Pennsylvania Railroad, fondly known as the "Ma and Pa," was just 77 miles long, connecting Baltimore, Maryland, and York, Pennsylvania, so it rarely acquired a new locomotive. When it did present specifications to a builder, they were invariably modest, as compact Consolidation no. 43, built by Baldwin in 1925, clearly shows. Still, the seemingly unembellished 2–8–0 was a contradiction of sorts; while it sported a feedwater heater and pump (to preheat the water before admitting it to the boiler, greatly increasing thermal efficiency), the tender rode on long-obsolete arch-bar trucks. The Ma and Pa maintained its humble country ways through the 1960s, when prominent railway preservationist George Hart ran several of his steam locomotives on the bucolic, and by then freight-only, little line.

Compound Mallets in the 2–4–4–2 and 0–6–6–0 and especially the 2–6–6–2 configuration were popular for heavy log trains on relatively well-maintained main lines of
some of the larger lumber companies, including Rayonier and Weyerhauser, both of
which utilized them into the 1960s in the Pacific Northwest. Insular Lumber Company's 0–6–6–0 no. 7, turned out by Baldwin's Eddystone Works in 1925, was a typical
logging heavy-hauler. Her "cabbage" stack housed an elaborate netting spark arrester to
ensure that sparks from her wood fire would not set her owner's valuable timberland
ablaze. The six-wheel tender was a rare feature on a twentieth-century American
locomotive, giving her much more of a European or Far Eastern appearance. This side
view offers ample basis for comparison between the huge low-pressure cylinders and the
smaller high-pressure ones. Normally, larger logging engines, such as this one, carried
timber from the loaders or spur-line junctions to the mill on more or less permanent
track. The branch lines, which were often moved to follow the logging crews, were
usually much cruder in construction, with sharp curves and undulating, ungraded
track, requiring smaller engines or even geared ones, which were much less prone to
derailing under such circumstances.

81

Insular Lumber
Company No. 7

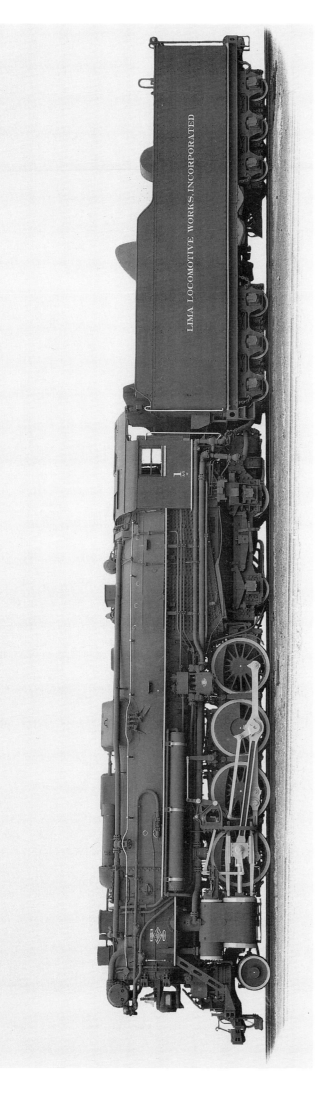

82

Lima Locomotive Works No. 1

When a technology evolves slowly and methodically, not spurred on by urgency (such as that of a war for national survival), it is difficult to pinpoint quantum advances. Rather, each new variant shows minor improvements over previous models. The development of the steam locomotive is a good example of the steady, albeit slow, forward march of engineering progress, even early in the twentieth century, when the tempo of advancement accelerated. If, however, there ever was a single steam locomotive that could be called "revolutionary" and a "breakthrough," it was the first "super-power" engine, the Lima Locomotive Works' 2–8–4 of 1925. With an enormous steam generator of a boiler and a firebox so big that it required—for the first time—a four-wheel trailing truck for support, this "A-1" locomotive was built by Lima on its own—an early example of risking valuable time and capital on a purely speculative venture. The executives of the railroad industry watched Lima's A-1 much as the airlines were to

view the Boeing 707 jet some thirty-odd years later—with great interest and wide-open checkbooks. Lima sent its masterpiece barnstorming across American railroads and filled its order books. The Boston & Albany tested this radical 2–8–4, then ordered an incredible total of 55, naming the type the "Berkshire"—after the mountains in western Massachusetts that the A-1 had so handily conquered. The Illinois Central followed, buying fifty more. By the time the last one was turned out by Lima in 1949, over six hundred 2–8–4s had been placed in main-line service in the U.S.A. In most instances, the Berkshires could haul trains whose weight and speed were increased at least 25 percent over those of the 2–8–2s and 2–8–0s they replaced; in some cases they doubled the speed, from thirty to over sixty m.p.h. Lima's bold venture in designing, building and promoting the first heavy-horsepower locomotive paid off handsomely for the company.

83

Texas & Pacific
Railway No. 600

So successful was Lima's A-1 2–8–4 that within months the company's design staff enlarged it by adding a driving axle to create the 2–10–4. This modification was a response to a request from the Texas & Pacific for an engine that could haul heavier trains at a moderate increase in speed over the rolling hills and valleys of the Lone Star State. The prototype, no. 600, was the first truly modern 2–10–4, and it radically altered the operations of the T. & P. Not an especially large road, the Texas & Pacific operated entirely within the state of its corporate title, plus Louisiana, and never came close to reaching the Pacific Ocean. Still, it carried much traffic and, with the 1920s boom, needed heavier power, but shied from articulated engines. Like many railroads that originated a locomotive type, T. & P. went on to purchase more 2–10–4s (seventy) than any other road (except the Pennsylvania, which erected 125 of them during 1942–43); by World War II, the 2–10–4s handled virtually all of its manifest freights. Much larger railroads (Chesapeake & Ohio, Pennsy, Santa Fe), as well as smaller roads, also rostered fleets of 2–10–4s, but the T. & P. was the first and it gave the type its name—the "Texas,"—that was to gain it international renown. Within a decade, the 2–10–4 grew vastly in size (T. & P. 600s weighed 448,000 pounds and rode on 63-inch driving wheels; the Santa Fe versions were almost fifty tons heavier in engine weight and had incredibly high 74-inch drivers), becoming one of the most successful of modern steam designs. Texas & Pacific no. 610—the only one of the nine surviving North American 2–10–4s of the original design—was restored to active service and ran for five years in the 1976–81 period. Although relatively few examples are left, the great locomotive known as the Texas will be remembered as long as men gather to reminisce about the golden age of steam railroading.

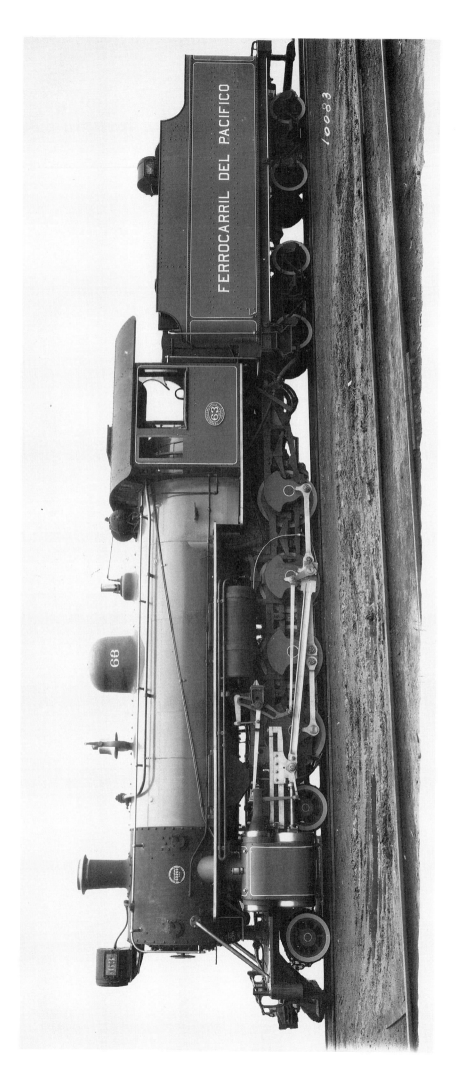

Ferrocarril del Pacífico No. 63

Although occasionally handsome, most heavy-duty narrow-gauge steam engines invariably exuded a squat look, no matter what their wheel arrangement may have been. This aesthetics problem was mostly due to the circumstance that while the boiler, cylinders, cab and perhaps the tender tank often matched harmoniously, the wheels were usually in the forty- to fifty-inch-diameter range, giving them an incorrigible look of hunkered-down squatness. To allow for a larger and heavier design, the frames were placed outside of the driving wheels, but inside the counterweights and machinery. The result was that the wheels were almost completely hidden from view, as was the case with Ferrocarril del Pacífico 4–8–0 no. 63, an otherwise pleasant three-foot-gauge locomotive of average size, constructed by Baldwin in 1927.

85

Manila Railway No. 144

During the century of colonial empires, when the mother countries built railroads in their colonies they typically sold the colonists the rolling stock and other equipment as well. It was therefore quite natural that Baldwin of Philadelphia supplied most of the locomotives exported to the Philippines after the United States liberated that vast archipelago during the Spanish–American War in 1898. The Manila Railway on Luzon was the largest common-carrier operation; most other lines served the sugar plantations and some remained in steam into the 1980s—decades after the Manila Railway had dieselized. Handsome Pacific no. 144, built by Baldwin in 1927, was a thoroughly modern locomotive, complete with Worthington feedwater heater and piston-valve cylinders.

Atchison, Topeka & Santa Fe Railway No. 3450

The Atchison, Topeka & Santa Fe ordered its first 4–6–4 shortly after the prototype was built for the New York Central in 1927. While most Hudsons were graceful and nimble in appearance, the overbearing size of modern A.T. & S.F. steam locomotives made even the 4–6–2s and 4–6–4s of that road look more like freight haulers than the 110-m.p.h. passenger power they were. In fact, so large were Santa Fe's Hudsons, as typified by the 3450, that they even dwarfed their original twelve-wheel tenders and, when it came to sheer strength, rivaled many other roads' 4–8–2s and 4–8–4s in weight. (Although the 3450s were large, the 3460s, built by Baldwin a decade later, were immense, weighing even more than the Richmond, Fredericksburg & Potomac's 4–8–4s!) Because of operating practices dating back to Civil War–era 4–4–0s, many railway motive-power departments never fully appreciated the potential of the modern super-power

passenger locomotive and continued to insist on changing engines on long-distance trains every 200–400 miles. Not so the Santa Fe, which ran its oil-fired Hudsons and Northerns for distances of over 1,200 to almost 1,800 miles without change and could even make a Hudson go all the way from Chicago to Los Angeles (2,200 miles) on schedule, then service the engine and send it back two hours later! Other Western roads made impressive runs (the Northern Pacific had the longest coal-fired district in the world, with its 4–8–4s going 1,008 miles), but none matched the A.T. & S.F. for the consistent length of its runs and the weight and speed of the trains on its crack passenger schedules. With the exception of the Norfolk and Western and perhaps the New York Central, no railroad sought to exploit the true potential of the last-generation steam locomotive as did the Atchison, Topeka & Santa Fe.

87
Baldwin
Locomotive Works
No. 60000

By 1927, the Baldwin Locomotive Works' design staff had developed the plans for a high-pressure water-tube boiler, but no railroad was interested in paying to have such a radically new engine built, so the final drawings were made and sent to the erecting shop, and the locomotive was built at Baldwin's expense. At the time, Baldwin was on the verge of building its sixty-thousandth locomotive, so the order in which the builder's plates were affixed to new boilers was jiggled a bit, and the big experimental 4–10–2 emerged from the factory bearing not only builder's number 60000, but that road number as well. Heralded by much fanfare and media publicity, the locomotive barnstormed around the country, being tested on scores of railroads. Unfortunately the Great Depression soon began to wreak havoc with the national economy, greatly exacerbating the usual problem encountered by radically new design concepts: resistance to the status quo by railway motive-power departments. After four years, in which the 60000 proved successful in generating steam but not in generating duplicate orders, she was donated to the Franklin Institute in Philadelphia—the city of her birth—and there she remains, on display inside.

88
Boston and Maine
Railroad No. 4000

Seeing the success of the Boston & Albany in the utilization of its Lima Berkshires, neighbor Boston and Maine bought 25 copies in 1928 and '29. Because of more restrictive clearances, the B. and M. engines were equipped with Coffin feedwater heaters; normally built inside the smokebox, these had to be mounted in front of the locomotive, creating a dark, cluttered and unusually weird appearance. The eighty 2–8–4s purchased by the Boston & Albany and Boston and Maine were paradoxical: they represented the bulk of modern steam power that was to be acquired by railroads of New England, despite the fact that these were the railroads that had heralded the birth of the super-power era on U.S. roads. After this sudden burst of activity in the late twenties, only a few more steam locomotives were bought by either the two Berkshire buyers or the other New England systems. Most were content to steam into post–World War II dieselization with World War I locomotive rosters.

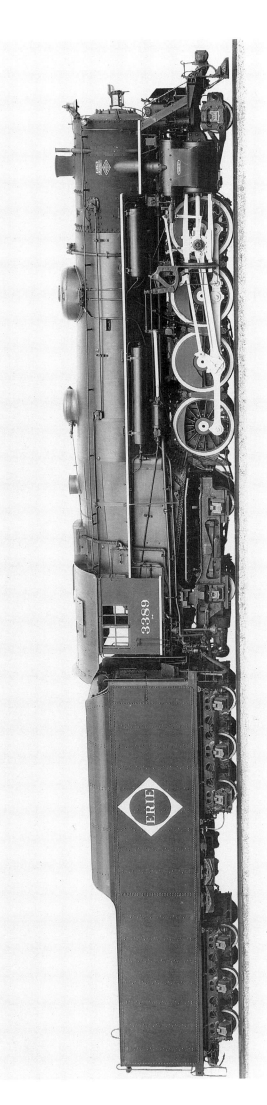

89

Erie Railroad No. 3389

Even more dramatic than the sudden influx of 2–8–4 Berkshires into New England from 1925 through 1929 was the simultaneous acquisition by the Erie Railroad of 105 nearly identical locomotives. With this vast number, Erie became the greatest of all 2–8–4 operators. Its investment paid off, for the company needed no additional motive power until dieselization, nearly a quarter-century later. So impressed was the Erie with the Berkshire that it turned to Alco and Baldwin, as well as Lima, to crank out as many as possible as quickly as possible.

Somewhat similar to the builder portrait in concept and purpose, if not in technique, was the railroad-company publicity photograph. A photographer—often a full-time employee—would pose an entire train on an especially suitable or scenic section of the right-of-way and expose several eight-by-ten-inch negatives from various angles, then submit prints to the management for consideration. Sometimes, a photo—like this one taken around 1930 of New York Central 4-6-4 Hudson no. 5271 and a train of ten heavyweight cars—was especially appealing and would result in hundreds of prints being distributed to newspapers and magazines. This picture showed off not only a first-class train but Central's renowned four-track "Water-Level Route" as well. (*Ron Ziel Collection.*)

90
New York Central Railroad No. 5271

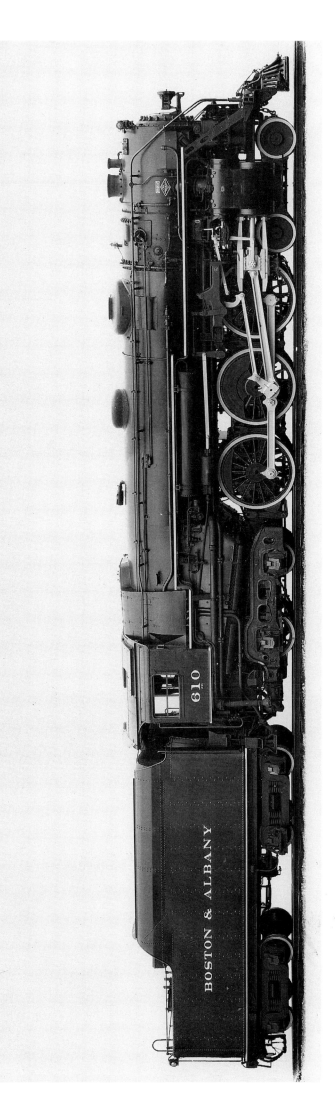

91
Boston & Albany
Railroad No. 610

Several years after the New York Central introduced the 4–6–4, its subsidiary, the Boston & Albany, ordered slightly modified copies for its heavier passenger runs, including the Boston section of the Twentieth Century Limited, which was combined with (or separated from) the namesake train at Albany, New York. The main difference in the B. & A. version was the substitution of 75-inch driving wheels for the parent road's 79-inch size—a seemingly minor alteration that nevertheless proved vital in moving heavy Pullman trains over the Berkshire Mountains. The B. & A. Hudsons also had much smaller tenders than the prototypes; in all other respects, they were of the same superb tradition that gained the Central's J-class 4–6–4 the distinction of being probably the single most acclaimed passenger locomotive in the entire history of railroading. Unfortunately, all of New York Central's 275 Hudsons—plus the Boston & Albany versions—were cut up for scrap. In the 1990s, serious consideration is being given to raising a million dollars or so to have an exact operating replica built in Poland!

92
Nickel Plate Road
No. 177

After the 4–6–4 passenger locomotive was developed for the New York Central in 1927, other railroads began ordering the Hudson type. Among the earlier purchasers was the New York, Chicago & St. Louis (Nickel Plate Road), which placed in service a design of such modest proportions that it was more like a Pacific with a four-wheel trailing truck. Its 73-inch driving wheels were among the smallest on any 4–6–4 and the trailing truck appears almost to have been squeezed beneath the firebox; but the NKP ran modest passenger trains on moderate schedules, so even a small Hudson was an improvement over the predecessors it replaced.

93
Royal State
Railways of Siam

During the late 1920s, Baldwin built a batch of three-cylinder Pacifics for the Royal State Railways of Siam. When the author saw them there 45 years later, they had undergone less change, over so long a time period, than virtually any other class of locomotive ever built! Except for conversion from arrow-drop couplers to American-style knuckle couplers and a change in the company title from Siam to Thailand, these 4–6–2 wood-burners were running practically as built. The third cylinder was cast into the saddle right between the two outer ones; when working these engines made an uncanny off-beat exhaust racket that can only be described as sounding like a four-cylinder articulated that had one set of driving wheels slipping and out of synchronization. The Baldwins performed well and most survived the Japanese occupation and World War II, but by 1974 virtually all were retired.

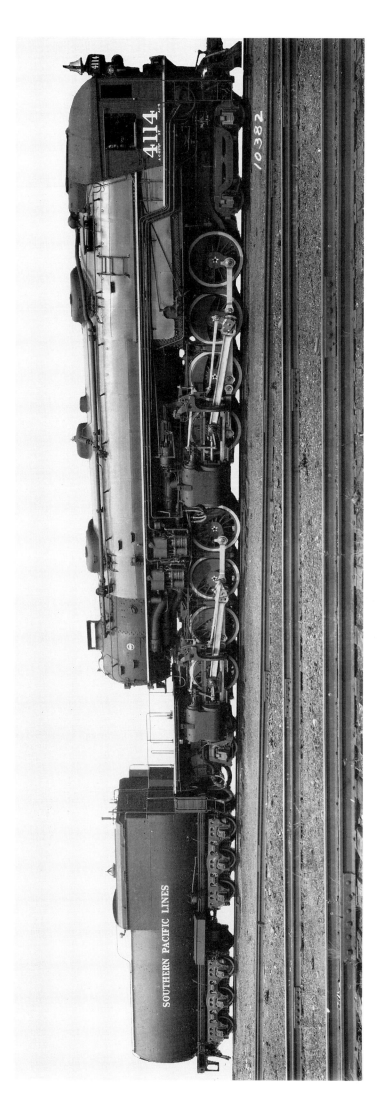

94

Southern Pacific Lines No. 4114

The most distinctive locomotive design since the nineteenth-century camelback was the renowned cab-forward, 195 of which were built by Baldwin for the Southern Pacific over a period of sixteen years, beginning in 1928. The idea of flipping a huge locomotive around to operate backward was conceived as the only practical solution to the problem of the near-asphyxiation of engine crews in the long snowsheds and tunnels of the Sierra Nevada Mountains in California. As for visibility for the crews, the Espee locomotives were unmatched by any other steam design anywhere. Oil burning made possible the separation of the firebox from the tender by sixty feet of boiler and frame; no workable stoker could have been designed to push coal that distance. With a relatively few simple modifications (enclosing the cab, piping the oil and water along the length of the engine),

it was easy to modify the basic 2–8–8–4 heavy freight locomotive for this service, which saw the S.P. running them on passenger trains as well. Railway historians who should know better refer to these locomotives as "the only 4–8–8–2s ever built"—a ridiculous conclusion, since merely running an engine backward with the tender coupled to the front hardly alters its wheel arrangement! All sorts of rare and exotic types of locomotives could be concocted merely by taking any of an existing type and doing what Espee did. A more accurate designation for the type would be 2–8–8–4R (for "Reverse"). Only one of the huge Articulated-Consolidations (or "A-Cs", as S.P. classified them) survives—no. 4294, the last new steam locomotive purchased by the Southern Pacific, in 1944—in restored splendor at the California State Railroad Museum in Sacramento.

95

Alton and Southern Railroad No. 14

The Alton and Southern was a switching line. As such, it operated shunting locomotives that were larger and more powerful than many main-line long-distance heavy freight-haulers. Forming a rough, undulating one-third circle in Illinois, across the Mississippi River from St. Louis, Missouri, the A. and S. interchanged with 22 other railroads along its less than fifty miles of track. This 0–10–0, no. 14, outshopped by Baldwin in 1930, was a fine specimen of the very heavy modern switch engine, complete with two cross-compound air compressors and a huge tender that featured a booster engine to assist in starting the heaviest trains. Indeed, this tender was more suited to a road engine of 2–10–2 proportions than even the road switcher that no. 14 was.

96

Durham and
Southern Railroad
No. 200

Although the 2–10–0 Decapod never gained the widespread acceptance in North America that it was to know in much of Europe, the Middle East and Russia, there were some fine examples acquired by U.S. railroads, big and small. While few were to be ordered by domestic lines after 1925, those that were, such as no. 200 of the 57-mile Durham and Southern in North Carolina, were usually handsome machines. Built by Baldwin in 1930, this typical Decapod featured an extremely high-riding boiler that showed a lot of daylight above the wheels, on account of the necessity of having to carry a relatively deep and wide firebox over the rear drivers. Had this engine been a comparable-size 2–8–2, the boiler could have been lowered almost two feet. It is interesting also to note how little bearing surface there was between the massive boiler and the carrying frame of a steam locomotive, a phenomenon accented by high-boilered engines such as no. 200. Because of heat expansion (under steam, the steel expanded considerably from when the locomotive was cold), the only rigid, inflexible mounting was up front, on the cylinder saddle. The plate, visible endwise between the third and fourth wheels, bent ever so slightly as the boiler expanded above the cold frame. The firebox rested on a grooved surface in the frame, which allowed it to move lengthwise but not laterally.

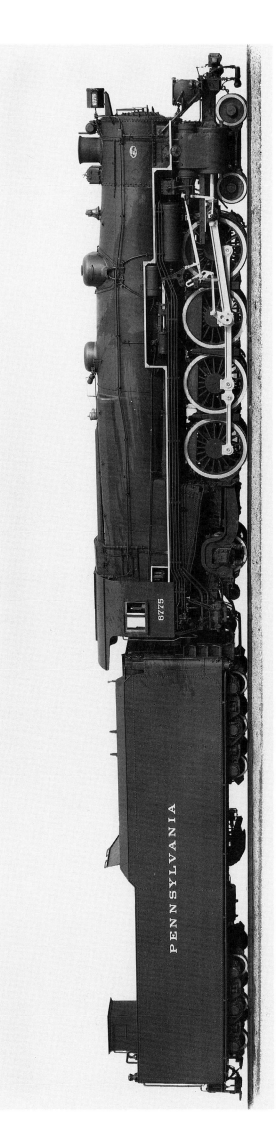

97
Pennsylvania Railroad No. 6775

Compared to a 4–8–2 of less than ten years earlier, such as Great Northern no. 1755 (photo 62, above), the Pennsylvania Railroad's own design of the Mountain type was a great advance. With driving wheels an even six feet in diameter (ten inches more than those of the G. N. engine), the M-1 was truly a dual-service machine. In fact, the Pennsy applied pilots with utilitarian footboards to the ones assigned to freight duties and passenger pilots to those in passenger service. The prototype was built in 1923 and, by 1930, three hundred duplicates had been ordered. Most were turned out by the Pennsy's own shops in Altoona but the final hundred came from Baldwin. One of the latter was no. 6775, one of the engines to be built with an enormous tender that was equipped with a scoop for taking water at fifty m.p.h. while hauling the Pennsy's premier passenger runs. Referred to as an "ocean-to-ocean" tender by P.R.R. crews, it carried enough coal to run over three divisions without stopping. Among the most famous of Pennsy power, the M-1 lasted until the end of steam in 1957. Only one of the 301 engines survives—with its big tender—at the Pennsylvania State Railroad Museum in Strasburg.

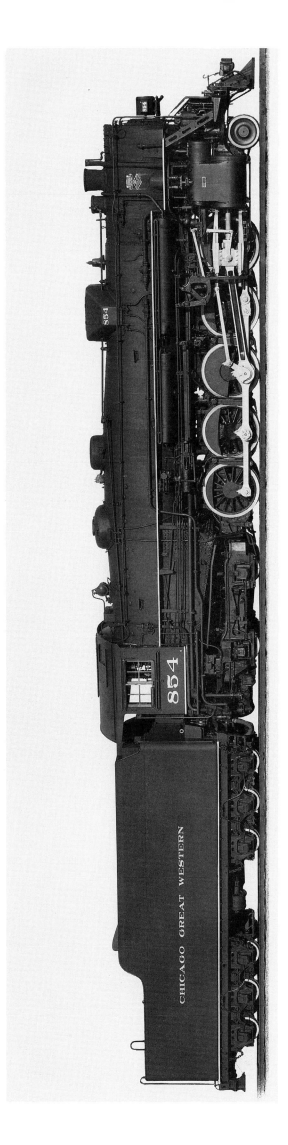

98

Chicago Great
Western Railroad
No. 854

The Chicago Great Western, like the Texas & Pacific, was a moderate-size line that went for the 2–10–4 in a big way, ordering 36 of them in 1930. Virtually identical with the T. & P. prototypes in size, weight, performance and appearance, the C.G.W. engines worked grain trains and mixed freight in the granger lands of the Midwest. The one drawback of the early 2–10–4s was their comparatively small-diameter 63-inch driving wheels, which generally held them down to speeds below fifty m.p.h. Texas types of the 1930s, such as those of the Kansas City Southern, with 70-inch drivers, and Santa Fe, with 74-inch drivers, easily topped sixty m.p.h. both on fast freights and—when required—on the heaviest passenger moves, especially World War II troop trains.

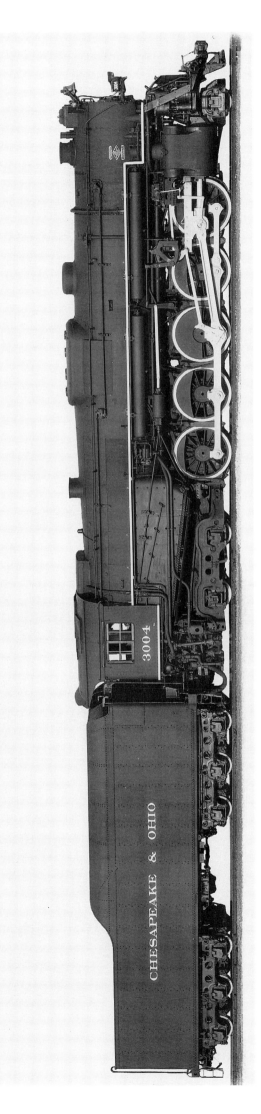

99

Chesapeake & Ohio Railway No. 3004

When Chesapeake & Ohio presented its specifications for forty 2–10–4s to Lima in 1930, their design required a larger boiler, cast trailing truck and other refinements that resulted in a free-steaming locomotive that was to become perhaps the most handsome of all the Texas types. That the engine was sound was borne out twelve years later when the Pennsylvania Railroad, banned by wartime restrictions from introducing new designs, ordered 125 locomotives based on the Chessie T-1 of 1930. Yet, when the C. & O. dieselized in the mid-fifties, it haphazardly preserved over twenty steam locomotives, including a dozen 2–8–4s—but not a single 2–10–4!

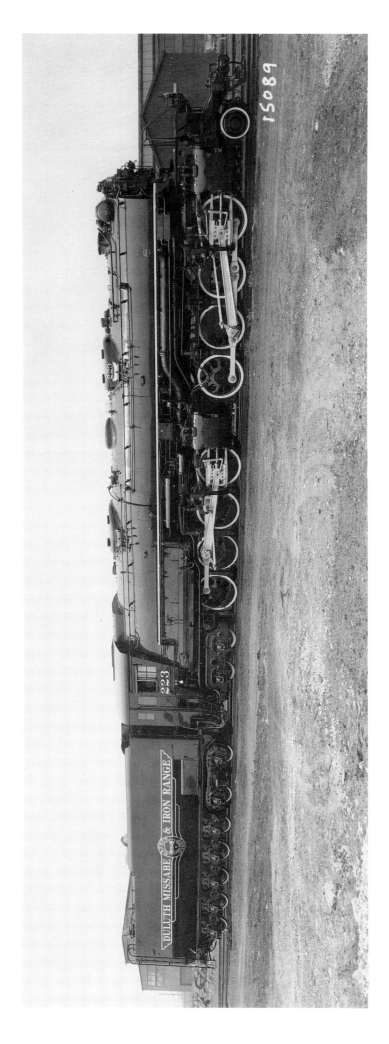

100

Duluth, Missabe & Iron Range Railroad No. 223

When the Northern Pacific originated the 2–8–8–4 wheel arrangement in 1928 and named it "Yellowstone," after the national park that was served by N.P., the company laid claim to owning the world's largest steam locomotive, a title it held until the Union Pacific 4–8–8–4 appeared in 1941. Thereafter, several other heavy-hauling roads were to adopt the type, including the Southern Pacific, which ordered 205 of them, all but ten of which were of the famed cab-forward variety. Among the most impressive of the genre were the 200-series Yellowstones of the Duluth, Missabe & Iron Range, whose principal freight was iron ore carried from the mines of the Mesabi Mountains to the docks on Lake Superior in Minnesota. In the twilight of their careers, when most locomotives were downgraded to lighter duties, the tonnage ratings of D.M. & I.R.'s 2–8–8–4s were markedly *increased* and, as steam was phased out in the late 1950s, they were hauling the heaviest trains ever handled by a single-unit locomotive—up to 19,000 tons (almost half the weight of an

Iowa-class battleship)! And when the diesels finally completely displaced these remarkable steamers in 1960, it took five of them to perform the tasks of one Yellowstone. The only 2–8–8–4s to run in the East came very late—in fact they were actually unwanted by their owner, the Baltimore & Ohio. Desperately short of motive power by the peak World War II year of 1944, the B. & O. requested permission from the War Production Board to purchase twenty 5,400-horsepower diesels. Since diesels required more strategic materials than steam (e.g., copper), the request was denied, and 2–8–8–4s were ordered from Baldwin instead. The B. & O. EM-1 engines were powerful and handsome, but ran for only a little over a decade before all twenty were scrapped. Although B. & O. preserved a good sampling of its steamers, the management later regretted the oversight of not having saved a Yellowstone. Just four 2–8–8–4s survive, three from D.M. & I.R. and one cab-forward from Southern Pacific.

101

Lehigh Valley
Railroad No. 5101

The original 4–8–4 locomotive was purchased by the Northern Pacific Railway, so the type was henceforth known as the "Northern" on most railroads. When the Lehigh Valley began to amass an impressive fleet of 55 4–8–4s in the 1930s, it named the class after a region in upstate New York traversed by L.V.'s mainline. The name chosen, "Wyoming," seemed much more appropriate to the Union Pacific, more than half a continent westward! No. 5101, built in 1934, was intended neither for passenger nor even for dual service as were most 4–8–4s; with her relatively low seventy-inch driving wheels, footboard pilot and booster on the rear tender truck, this early Wyoming was assigned to heavy freight work only.

102

Pittsburgh and
West Virginia
Railroad No. 1101

At a time when articulated locomotives were growing in size (from 0-6-6-0 in 1903 to 2-8-8-4 by 1928) and power, the trend was temporarily reversed when, in 1935, the Pittsburgh and West Virginia and the Seaboard Air Line both ordered different versions of the 2-6-6-4 wheel arrangement. Relatively small, but with a more ample firebox than their predecessor, the 2-6-6-2, these were the first dual-service four-cylinder simple locomotives. While primarily freight haulers, they could also keep heavy passenger trains to schedule. The P. & W.V. machines were of interest because of their square Belpaire fireboxes, which gave them a decidedly Pennsylvania Railroad appearance. The apex of this rare type (only three railroads used them)

came with the development of Norfolk and Western's Class-A 2-6-6-4 in the early 1940s. A superb steamer, riding on seventy-inch driving wheels, the "A" had no problem topping seventy m.p.h. on level stretches of the N. & W. with a hundred cars of merchandise or holiday-swollen passenger extras and troop trains. Only one 2-6-6-4 survives: N. & W. no. 1218, restored to active service in 1987. She runs thousands of miles in scores of excursions annually as the second-largest steam locomotive running in the world in the 1990s. The trend towards larger articulated power resumed in 1936 with the development of Union Pacific's 4-6-6-4, and culminated in the 2-6-6-6 and 4-8-8-4 types in 1941.

The 4–8–0 twelve-wheeler enjoyed only modest acceptance both in the United States and worldwide; consequently just four are known to survive in North America: one Southern Pacific and three Norfolk & Western (one of the latter was acquired by the Strasburg Rail Road in 1991 and was to be restored to operation in its own shops). The last 4–8–0s to run in regular service on the continent were a batch of modern engines built for the Ferrocarriles Nacionales de México in 1935—a late date, indeed, for a type long considered obsolete. The prototype, no. 3000, was the one selected by Baldwin for the official portrait. The author also managed to get one photograph of her under steam at the Valle de México terminal on his first visit there in 1962. Two years later, he photographed sister no. 3002, which had become the last 4–8–0 to operate in regular service in North America, as she pulled local freights on a daily basis north from Mexico City. All of the trim Mexican twelve-wheelers have long been scrapped, but their legacy will be preserved by ex–N. & W. no. 475 at Strasburg, although not nearly as well proportioned or handsome as her descendants that went south of the border.

103

Ferrocarriles Nacionales de México No. 3000

104
Union Railroad No. 303

When the term "modern" is used in reference to locomotives, switch engines rarely enter the equation, being relegated to the backwaters of engineering science. Yet many were state-of-the-art, and it is perhaps poetic justice that the last new steam locomotive to be bolted and welded together for a major U.S. carrier was a chunky 0–8–0, turned out by Norfolk and Western in December 1953. Switchers have always been thought of as much smaller than road engines, but, in 1936, Baldwin turned out five massive 0–10–2s for the Union Railroad that, at 404,000 pounds engine weight, were heavier than Canadian National 4–8–4s! Named the "Union" type, they were the only 0–10–2s ever built. After being transferred to another United States Steel company line—the Pittsburgh & Lake Erie—one of these rarities was preserved. (*Ron Ziel Collection.*)

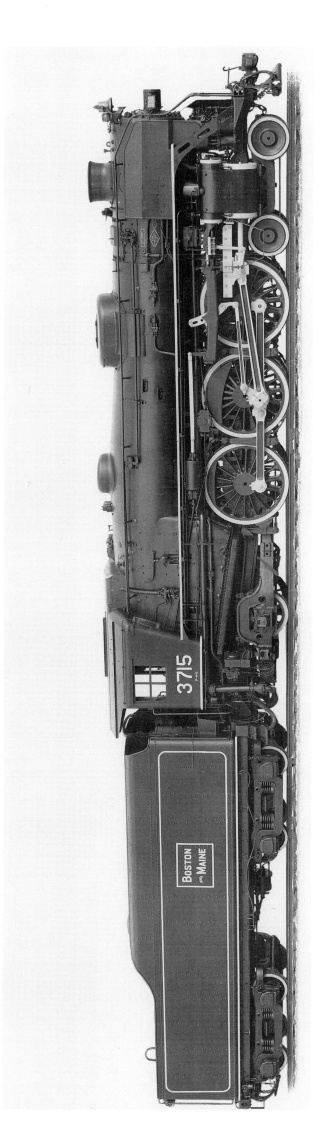

105
Boston and Maine
Railroad No. 3715

Almost a decade after most major railways stopped ordering 4–6–2s in favor of larger and more powerful 4–6–4s and 4–8–4s to haul their premier passenger trains, the Boston and Maine chose to acquire a series of heavy Pacifics. Although their eighty-inch driving wheels defined them as fast passenger power, they were also intended for priority merchandise service. Five were built in 1934 and another five in 1937. With their small smoke deflectors, rounded edges and most unsightly plumbing hidden from view, the P-4-b-class locomotives were recognized as being among the most handsome of 4–6–2s. Fortunately, the late F. Nelson Blount, founder of the Steamtown Museum (more recently the National Railroad Museum, in Scranton, Pennsylvania), saved one of them, and it is hoped that she may someday be made operational.

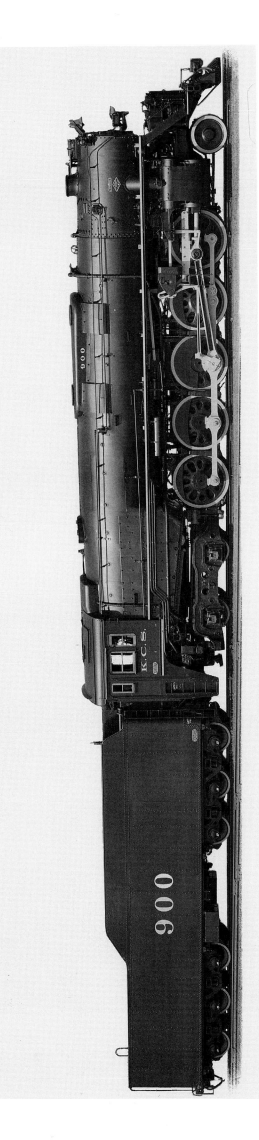

The ten 2–10–4s built by Lima for the Kansas City Southern in 1937 were illustrative of how quickly the Texas type had evolved since its genesis a little over a decade previously. While the original Texas & Pacific 2–10–4 (see photo 83, above) was an angular and somewhat clumsy machine that rode on low 63-inch driving wheels, the K.C.S. 900-series, although much larger and 36 tons heavier, with seventy-inch wheels, was possessed of a much cleaner, indeed, almost streamlined look, with its hidden piping, enclosed cab and combination steam dome and sandbox. Able to haul trains that formerly required the double-heading of 2–8–0s, and accomplishing the task at almost twice the speed, the 2–10–4s were favorites of both their crews and the cost-conscious management. Like most superb modern steam power, however, their service lives were cut short by decades when diesels arrived in numbers in the 1950s.

106

Kansas City Southern Railroad No. 900

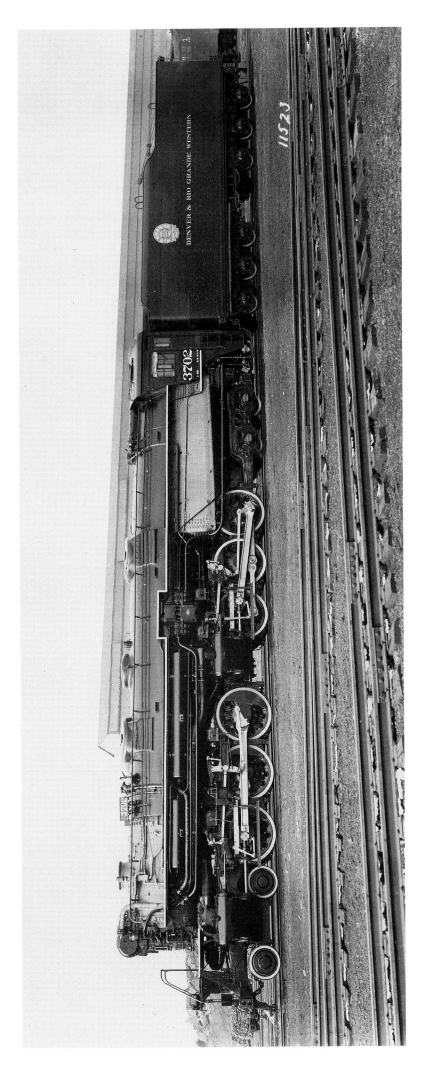

107

Denver & Rio Grande Western Railroad No. 3702

Articulated locomotives, with two sets of driving wheels (the front set, on its own frame, swiveling freely on a pin) powered by four cylinders, first appeared on the American railroad scene in the early 1900s. Originally, they were of the "Mallet" type (named for the French designer who originated the concept), a compound engine that used the steam twice by exhausting it from a pair of high-pressure cylinders into larger-diameter low-pressure ones. These locomotives, powerful but slow, were used mainly as helpers or to haul heavy drag freights up steep grades. By the late 1920s the four-high-pressure-cylinders engine had evolved, allowing a more powerful and faster (though less economical) updating of Mallet's design. Except for maverick Norfolk and Western, which continued to build huge compound

2–8–8–2s until 1952, few railroads bought compounds after 1930. With its clean lines, seventy-inch driving wheels and glistening surface, Denver & Rio Grande Western 4–6–6–4 no. 3702 looked like a passenger engine when new at Baldwin in 1937. The appearance was not deceptive, for the Challenger type, which had been originated by the Union Pacific just the previous year, was considered a dual-service engine, being comfortable with a fast merchandise train or twenty Pullmans. The Northern Pacific, as well as the D. & R.G.W. and U.P., often used its 4–6–6–4s in passenger service—most notably on troop trains, where they could match the speed of 4–8–4s on grades and reach for seventy miles per hour on flat terrain.

108
New York, New Haven & Hartford Railroad No. 1408

Since much of the main line of the New York, New Haven & Hartford ran along the coast of Long Island Sound, it was known as the "Shore Line," the name given to the ten conservatively—yet elegantly—streamlined 1-5 4–6–4s built by Baldwin in 1937. With a minimum of white striping and white driving-wheel centers and tires, the 1400-series locomotives were to be the only really streamlined steam engines to run in New England. (Rutland slapped some sheet metal on an old 2–8–0, but this hardly qualifies as the genuine article.) They easily replaced aged double-heading Pacifics on such crack varnish as the Merchants Limited, between Boston and New Haven, where electrics took over for the run to Grand Central Terminal in Manhattan. Although bumped by diesels after only fifteen years, they won a final victory: their replacements could not keep the heaviest trains on schedule, so a few 1-5s remained a little longer, until internal-combustion reinforcements arrived! (Ron Ziel Collection.)

Eleven years after it ordered the world's first 4–6–4, New York Central turned to the American Locomotive Company's Schenectady Works, located along its main line, for a truly remarkable improvement in the original design to produce the "Super Hudson" of 1938, which boasted a 25 percent increase in power at seventy m.p.h. The last ten were streamlined by leading industrial designer Henry Dreyfuss with a tasteful shrouding, skyline casing and bullet nose with a vertical fin that heralded the space age in line and form. In addition, these "Super-Duper" 4–6–4s were given roller bearings on all axles and rods and rode on Scullin disc driving wheels, which were cast almost solid, with just a few small holes, to reduce dynamic augment—the pounding of the rails at high speed. And speed they did, at the head end of what many historians regarded as the world's greatest train, the Twentieth Century Limited, reducing its running time for the 960-mile New York-to-Chicago sprint from eighteen hours to just sixteen and a half—an incredible average speed of almost sixty miles per hour! (*Ron Ziel Collection.*)

109

New York Central Railroad No. 5453

110

Atchison, Topeka &
Santa Fe Railway
No. 5004

Only the Atchison, Topeka & Santa Fe would have the audacity to specify 74-inch driving wheels on a ten-coupled freight locomotive, larger than the drivers on some 4–6–2 passenger engines! Although it looked much larger, at an engine weight of 273 tons, A.T. & S.F.'s 2–10–4 design actually weighed less than the 69-inch- and 70-inch-drivered Texas types of the similarly conceived classes adopted by the Chesapeake & Ohio and the Pennsylvania. By any measurement, the Santa Fe 2–10–4s were big and powerful and capable of wheeling perishable and other premier freight at speeds unattainable by any other ten-drivered locomotive. Just seven Texas types were pre-served in the United States, five of them by the Santa Fe.

An adjunct to the builder portrait was the "rebuilder portrait," commemorating a railroad's modernizing of an older locomotive to upgrade it for years—perhaps decades—of extended service, sometimes in a completely new role. In this context, a railway might amputate the pilot axle of a 2–8–0 road engine, which would emerge as an 0–8–0 switcher, or a heavy decade-old 4–6–2 might receive a larger firebox and become a 4–6–4. Illinois Central rebuilt drag-freight 2–10–2s into fast 4–8–2s, and Reading actually used boilers and other components of huge 2–8–0s in an ambitious (and very successful) program to enlarge the 2–8–0s into a roster of thirty 4–8–4s. In the late thirties, the St. Louis–San Francisco (Frisco Lines) took a tentative step into the streamlining craze, utilizing little more than some sheet metal and bright paint, when it gussied up 4–6–4 no. 1065; a set of Boxpok wheels replaced the original spoked main drivers to improve balance. "Rebuilding" a locomotive could mean anything from replacing the running gear to virtually jacking up the bell and rolling a whole new engine under it! (*Ron Ziel Collection.*)

111
———
*Frisco Lines
No. 1065*

112

Southern Pacific
Lines No. 3800

Despite the affinity of the Southern Pacific for cab-forward power (S.P. rostered nearly two hundred backward-running articulateds), in 1939 the company purchased a dozen conventional 2–8–8–4s, built as coal burners to take advantage of cheap fuel from its own mines. Streamlining was difficult to accomplish on so large an articulated, but by applying a solid pilot, "skyline" casing above the boiler and a smooth-lined cab, and concealing much of the piping beneath the jacketing, a semistreamlined effect was achieved that greatly enhanced the appearance of these AC-9 locomotives. Late in their careers, Espee transferred the big Yellowstones to California and converted them to oil-burners, but never went the final step of flipping the engines around and making them cab-forwards.

113

Pennsylvania Railroad No. 6100

The Pennsylvania Railroad, perhaps more than any other railway except Norfolk and Western, was wedded to coal for locomotive fuel, the result of tradition, the proximity of on-line mines and the fact that some of its biggest customers were shippers of the black "Pennsylvania real estate." By the late 1930s, steam traction was already locked in a battle for survival, pitted against the new, highly successful diesel road engines. Those committed to steam turned to radical concepts to outperform the challenger that was using internal combustion to power trains. For seven years (1938–45) the Pennsy worked with the major locomotive builders to design and erect a series of sensational and huge duplex-drive (four cylinders mounted on one rigid, nonarticulated frame) classes of engines. These were so extreme a departure from past practice that even their wheel arrangements were totally new. The first of these, no. 6100, the only 6–4–4–6 ever built, weighed 304 tons (more than a Western Maryland 4–6–6–4!), and, 140 feet from end to end, was the longest locomotive ever conceived. This was not a freight hog; with 84-

inch driving wheels, P.R.R.'s huge S-1 was intended solely for the fastest and heaviest passenger trains. No. 6100 gained instant fame when she was made into one of the most popular exhibits at the 1939–40 World's Fair in New York, where, under her own power, the driving wheels continuously turned as she sat stationary on sets of rollers. Too big to negotiate many curves or to ride virtually any turntables, she moved the Pennsy's name trains between Ohio and Chicago, frequently and easily surpassing a hundred miles per hour with 1,200-ton consists. Completely streamlined by noted industrial designer Raymond Loewy, the immense engine appeared to be doing a hundred even when standing still. Although an impressive performer, the S-1 was never duplicated. The P.R.R. also built duplex-drives in 4–6–4–4, 4–4–6–4 and 4–4–4–4 wheel arrangements (the latter two were produced only in limited numbers) for both passenger and freight duties; while some were successful, they all fell before the diesel onslaught by 1954. (*Ron Ziel Collection.*)

114
New York Central
Railroad No. 3037

The steam locomotives of the New York Central had a very distinctive, aristocratic appearance, as befits the company which, more than any other, prided itself on the excellence of its passenger service. In the latter days of the steam era, its great fleet of Hudsons and, for a brief season, its 4–8–4 Niagaras, powered such renowned trains as the Twentieth Century Limited, the Empire State Express, the Wolverine, the Lake Shore Limited and the Mercury. The third steed in Central's stable of thoroughbreds was the 4–8–2 Mohawk of L–3 and L–4 classes, built by Alco and Lima in the early 1940s. With 72-inch driving wheels they could keep the schedules with heavier sections of the name trains, as well as speeding manifest freights from St. Louis and Chicago to New York and back. The N.Y.C. even ran a fast merchandise train known as the Pacemaker and entrusted it to the speedy 4–8–2s, like no. 3037, shown here. Of modern Central steam, just two Mohawks survive, one of which—no. 3001—is being restored to operational status in Elkhart, Indiana.

115

Union Pacific
Railroad No. 3976

Articulated locomotives, with the front engine mounted on a separate frame, which was pivoted on the rigid frame that supported the boiler and carried the rear engine, were intended almost exclusively for freight service; the 4–6–6–4 Challenger, however, conceived by Union Pacific, was truly a dual-service engine. In fact, recalling that most quintessential of all passenger wheel arrangements, the 4–6–4 Hudson, it was not off target to refer to the 4–6–6–4 as a "double Hudson" when it was pulling a heavy passenger consist. It took the U.P. to assign certain Challengers specifically to passenger duties when, in the 1940s, it painted some of them in the two-tone gray with yellow striping that it used on its premier 800-series 4–8–4 "varnish" haulers. No. 3976, turned out by the American Locomotive Company's Schenectady Works in 1943, also, like the 800-series 4–8–4s, mounted passenger-style smoke lifters. The Challenger lived up to its romantic name by assaulting various ranges of the Rocky Mountains throughout Union Pacific territory, hauling heavy trains at timetable speeds. So successful was the design that in the final decade of mass-produced steam power, more Challengers were built than any other articulated type. With 105 4–6–6–4s in its stable, Union Pacific owned almost half of all built. At least six other roads—Denver & Rio Grande Western; Northern Pacific; Spokane, Portland & Seattle; Clinchfield; Western Maryland; and Delaware & Hudson—put the type to good use. Nearly extinct, just a pair of U.P. Challengers survives. No. 3977 is displayed at North Platte, Nebraska, and No. 3985 has run several times a year since its restoration by Union Pacific volunteers at the company's main shops in Cheyenne, Wyoming, in the early 1980s.

Union Pacific
Railroad No. 4002

In 1941, Union Pacific ordered what was to be the largest and heaviest (but not the most powerful) steam locomotive ever built. Within three years, the ALCO Schenectady Works in upstate New York turned out 25 of the immense brutes. Weighing nearly six hundred tons, including the fully loaded tender, the U.P. 4000-series locomotives were the only 4–8–8–4s ever built. They instantly became world famous, earning the company an enormous amount of publicity, as well as repaying its investment, by hauling the heaviest war freights as soon as they were delivered. Their service lives cut short by dieselization (it took five of the "growlers" to replace each 4000) by 1960, they nevertheless blast on in memory and legend. The U.P. had not coined a name for the type, basically an enlarged 4–6–6–4, when the first one arrived with the words "Big Boy" chalked on the smokebox. That name was just fine for Union Pacific's tastes and it stuck. This

photo of no. 4002, one of the original group, shows the locomotive articulating on a curve with its leading engine at an angle to the massive boiler. The whole machine dwarfs the engineer and fireman, who are comparing their pocket watches prior to taking the brand-new locomotive out on her first run (even Big Boy was referred to in the feminine gender) in a Union Pacific publicity photograph that deviates slightly from the stringent norms of the builder portrait. The American Locomotive Company (ALCO, which still builds diesel power) was an amalgamation of several independent United States and one Canadian builder, which united in 1901. The company went on to build more steam locomotives than Baldwin (almost eighty thousand), including some of the largest and finest, but the Rogers Collection, featured in this volume, displays mainly the workmanship of Baldwin and Lima—the two other major commercial steam-power builders.

117

**Boston and Maine
Railroad No. 4117**

In the tradition of the Pacifics it ordered in 1937, four years later the Boston and Maine bought some incredibly handsome 4–8–2 Mountain types, including no. 4117, for passenger and fast freight service, surprising perhaps, in view of the company's satisfaction with the extensive 2–8–4 roster it had acquired more than a decade earlier. Like most superb modern and efficient steam locomotives, they ran for all too short a time, their careers cut short by diesels less than fifteen years later, even as B. and M. 2–6–0s, built in the early 1900s, pulled commuter trains for over a half-century.

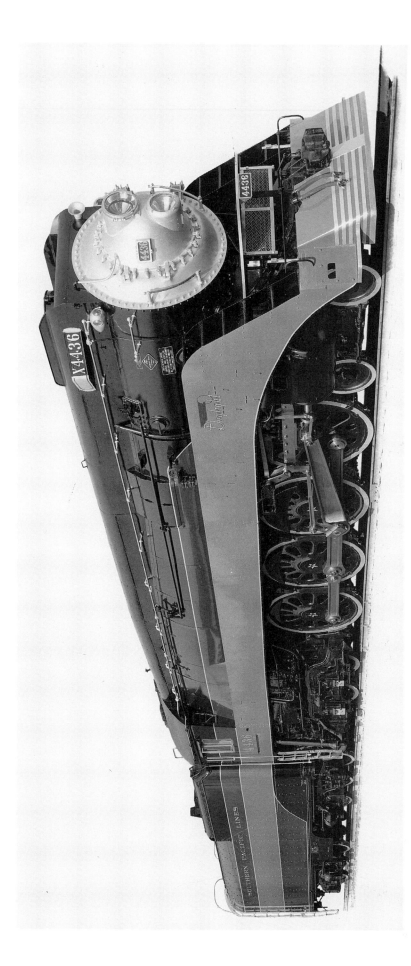

118

Southern Pacific Lines No. 4436

Among the earliest examples of true streamlining in the Art Deco era were the streamlined steam locomotives of 1934 and the streamlined Pioneer Zephyr, the first long-distance diesel train, introduced in the same year. Most of the earlier "streamlining" of steam locomotives consisted of applying what resembled an upside-down bathtub to almost completely cover the locomotive, a practice that was superficial and even ugly. It was also disastrous for maintenance, requiring the crews to unlatch and open access doors for even the simplest of servicing chores. Within a few years, the designers and railway officials realized that the locomotive itself was not something to be ashamed of and kept hidden from view; rather, its dynamic form and machinery could be enhanced by moderate applications of sheet metal and of paint other than the traditional glossy black. The result was some strikingly handsome adaptations, the most profound of which were the 4–6–4s of the New York Central's Twentieth Century Limited and the New York, New Haven & Hartford Railroad; the 4–8–4s originally designed for Southern Pacific Daylight service; and the 4–4–4–4 T-1 duplex-drive engines of the Pennsylvania Railroad. The secret of design behind these examples and a few others was that the streamlining was an integral part of the original design, rather than random claptrap

metal that was applied later by the shop forces. Indisputably, one of the most beautiful and successful results of streamlining was that of the Southern Pacific Daylight trains. Californians who witnessed the early runs of the red, orange and black consists immediately declared them to be "the most beautiful trains in the world," without fear of contradiction. The striping on locomotive and tender continued the length of the train and presented a bright, cheery image to a nation emerging from the Great Depression. Soon, the Daylight theme was applied to all of Espee's passenger liveries (except the drab commuter services) and lasted well into the diesel age. Lima built sixty Gs-class 4–8–4s, including ten stripped-down wartime versions, and the most renowned of them were nos. 4430–4449, erected in 1941. The last of these was the only streamlined one preserved (no. 4460 is also extant); after lying stationary for years in a museum in Portland, Oregon, she was resurrected in red, white and blue livery in 1975 to pull the American Freedom Train around the U.S.A. to commemorate the Bicentennial of American independence. Since then, the 4449 has been meticulously restored, including a complete matching train. It operates several times each year over much of the old Southern Pacific Lines, reviving the bright Daylight trains that were once the flagships of the S.P.

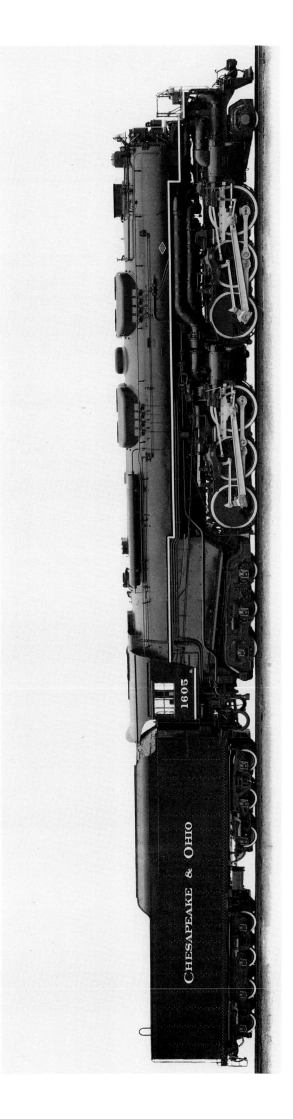

119

Chesapeake & Ohio
Railway No. 1605

When Chesapeake & Ohio wanted a heavy-horsepower freight engine capable of generating enormous reserves of steam, Lima designed a firebox so large and deep that it rode on a six-wheel trailing truck, completely aft of the driving wheels. The resulting 2–6–6–6 was so successful that, within a few years, the Chessie acquired a total of sixty of the behemoths, and nearby Virginian Railway ordered eight identical copies. Appropriately named "Allegheny," for the mountains they were built to conquer, the 2–6–6–6s were never driven to their full potential by the C. & O., which used them more often in slow coal-train service, a chore just as ably performed by low-drivered World War I–era compound 2–8–8–2s. By the time the last one was built in 1948, the Allegheny had earned a reputation for its brute strength, free steaming and availability and, when running a hundred-car merchandise train on level gradients, it could sustain sixty m.p.h. Like most of their modern steam contemporaries, these Chessie 1600s had their service lives abruptly cut short by the coming of the diesels. Two have been preserved.

Chesapeake & Ohio
Railway No. 246

The undue haste with which American railroads changed over from steam to diesel traction in the decade following World War II was never more dramatically demonstrated than by the Chesapeake & Ohio. During the 1940s, the C. & O. purchased more than two hundred new steam locomotives, ranging from 0–8–0s to 2–6–6–6–s, spending more than $40 million (well over a quarter-billion in 1991 dollars)—and retired all of them by 1957! The yard engines, exemplified by no. 246, that Lima built for the Chessie were so modern and efficient that neighboring Norfolk and Western, which prided itself on designing and building some of the finest of all steam power, was delighted to purchase the 0–8–0s when they were only a few years old at a bargain price of just $15,000 each. That the N. & W. was well satisfied with the almost-new shifters was shown when its own Roanoke Shops in Virginia built additional 0–8–0s to essentially the same Lima

designs. In fact, the final one was turned out in December 1953 as the last steam locomotive to be built in the United States for domestic use by a major railroad. (No new domestic steam was built here, but, over 35 years later, in 1989, several brand-new steam locomotives were imported from China.) Although the Chesapeake & Ohio was a major coal hauler, it had made the decision to dieselize during the prolonged 1949 coal miners' strike, thereby ensuring the early retirement of much of its finest steam power. N. & W. however, stayed with steam until the basic decision to change totally to diesels was made in 1957. Although it took C. & O. eight years to make the transformation, N. & W.—once the irrevocable decision had been made—went from 444 active steamers in 1957 to zero within just three years! This waste and haste led many railway economists to question the wisdom of so rapid a metamorphosis.

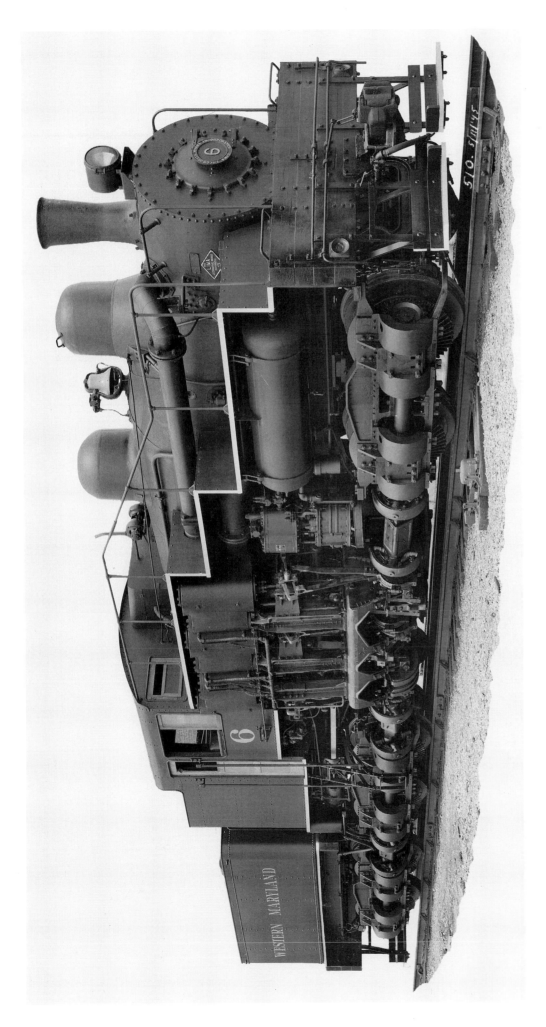

Western Maryland Railway No. 6

The biggest Shay was also the last one to be built by Lima, the company that was founded in the 1880s specifically to produce the unorthodox contraptions, then went on to design and build some of the largest and the best steam locomotives the world has ever known. As if that were not enough notoriety, 150-ton Shay no. 6 of the Western Maryland Railway, built in 1945, was one of the very few ever bought by a major line, rather than for industrial or logging use. After running only six years on a steeply graded mine branch, it was retired and donated to the B. & O. Railroad Museum. It has since been sent to the Cass Scenic Railway in West Virginia, where it has been fully restored to operation and runs several times annually. This photograph, more frontal than most builder shots, shows clearly the driving mechanism and gearing between the shaft and wheels. The larger Shays were three-truck models, with an auxiliary water tank supported by the third geared truck. No. 6 could pull any train that was coupled behind it—at about ten miles per hour!

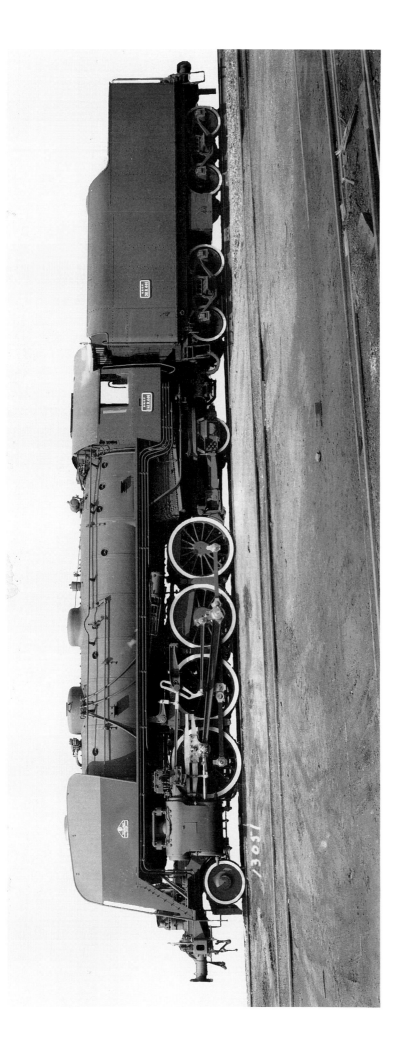

122

Société Nationale des Chemins de Fer Français 141.R No. 446

Among the most rakish and appealing of American export steam locomotives were the Liberation-class 2–8–2s built for the Société Nationale des Chemins de Fer Français (S.N.C.F.) between 1945 and 1947. More than four-fifths of the French National Railways' locomotives had been destroyed, severely damaged or expropriated by the Germans during the Second World War, so a massive infusion of new power was needed—and fast! The solution came quickly, in the form of the 141.R 2–8–2, 1,340 of which were erected by the three major U.S. builders, plus the Canadian Locomotive Works and Montreal Locomotive Company, in just two years. The French had been among the world's most successful steam-locomotive designers and builders, having created engines that were at once mechanically sophisticated and beautiful in line and form, but the motive-power crisis faced

by the S.N.C.F. at the time of Liberation was so severe that there was no time to work on new designs, so a very basic Mikado with medium-size driving wheels was chosen—a well-proven concept that was equally able to move heavy freights and hold down the schedules of all but the fastest express passenger trains. So successful was the 141.R type that, by 1951, although it comprised just 15 percent of the total locomotives on the S.N.C.F., it accounted for 30 percent of all engine-miles and handled 45 percent of all freight traffic, plus passenger runs. When the end of the steam era in France neared in 1971 and a mere five hundred steam locomotives remained on main-line French rails, over four hundred of the active engines were survivors of the once ubiquitous 141.R roster.

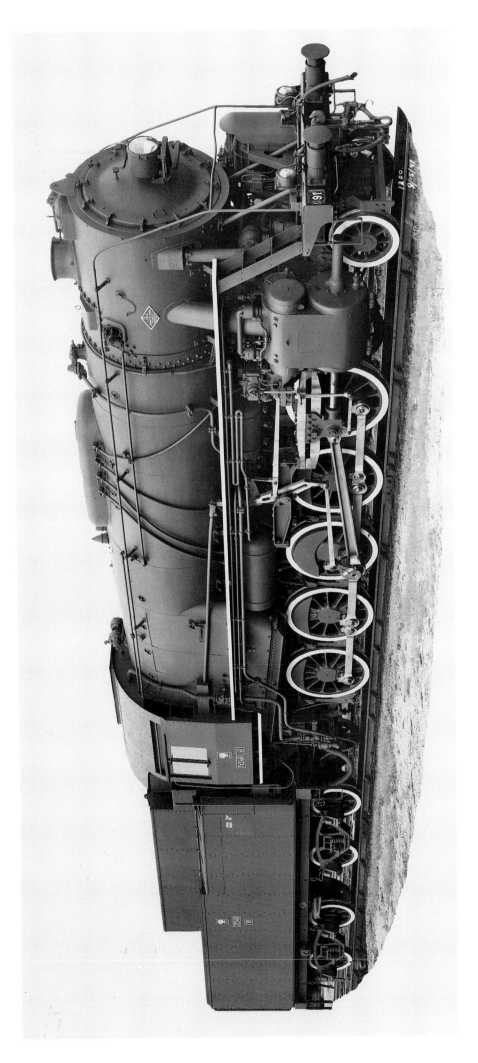

123

Polish State
Railways Ty246
No. 91

Among the thousands of locomotives representing hundreds of different designs that were exported from American manufacturers, few were as hulking and impressive-looking—or little known—as the one hundred 2–10–0 Decapods, designated class Ty246, built for the Polish State Railways in 1947. All three major builders erected the big engines and, no sooner had they been shipped to be unloaded in the port of Gdańsk when Stalin brought down the Iron Curtain and little was heard of the engines afterward. No. 91 was turned out by Lima on September 15, 1947, and, aside from the buffers and hook-and-link couplers, she would have looked right at home on many American railroads. A few survivors of the class were still running out of Malbork (the former German city of Marienburg) in 1974, when the author of this volume became one of the few Western photographers to be granted permission to engage in unhindered photography of Polish steam locomotives, including the Ty246s. Only two were found under steam, but the author was delighted, indeed, to have the opportunity to photograph even that pair! At least one has been preserved in the extensive museum collection of the Polish State Railways in Warsaw.

Chesapeake & Ohio
Railway No. 610

In the 1920s, the Lima Locomotive Works developed the concept of the "super-power" steam locomotive: a massive, sustained-capacity steam generator of a boiler, fired by a huge firebox carried on a four-wheel trailing truck. This immense power plant produced much more horsepower and higher efficiency than was previously attainable, greatly exalting the reputation of the company. Soon many of the leading U.S. railroads were ordering its products. By the 1940s, additional enhancements, such as roller bearings on all axles and rods, improved lubrication and other refinements, had brought the technology of the reciprocating steam locomotive to a peak of development. Among the very

sophisticated designs were the Chesapeake & Ohio J-3-a 4-8-4 Greenbrier types, the final five of which were built by Lima in 1948—just a year prior to the end of steam production. No. 610, first of the quintet, reveals the girth, the preponderance of modern appliances and the clean lines of the epitome of Lima super-power. Sister no. 614, the last of the batch, was saved from scrapping by the C. & O., and in the 1980s she operated quite a few excursions and even ran a series of tests on revenue coal trains to study the feasibility of reintroducing coal-fired locomotives on American railroads to ease the oil crisis. Stored serviceable as of this writing, the 614 may run again on Chessie rails.

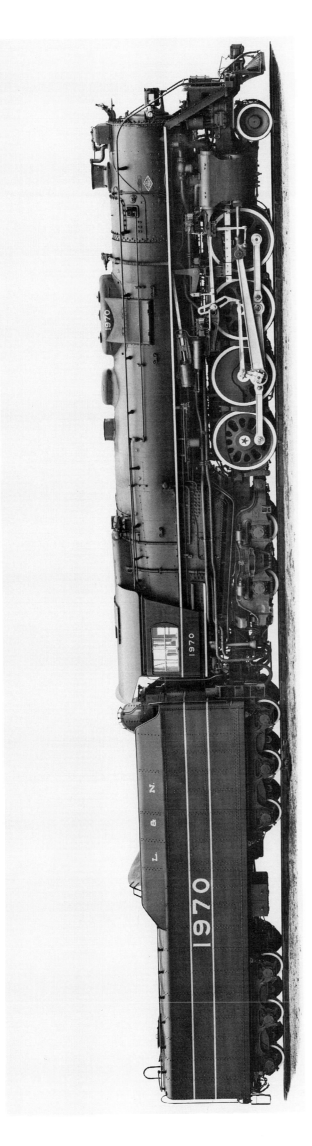

125

Louisville & Nashville Railroad No. 1970

The last sizable order of locomotives turned out by Lima prior to the final ten Berkshires for the Nickel Plate in 1949 consisted also of locomotives with the 2–8–4 wheel arrangement: 22 M-1-class engines for the Louisville & Nashville. Nos. 1970–1991 joined earlier identical sisters in their versatile roles of hauling everything from coal drags to express passenger trains. Fondly known as "Big Emma" to admiring crews, these last Berkshires survived less than eight years, before the L. & N.—the "Old Reliable"—was totally dieselized in January 1957. Only two smaller, older L. & N. steam engines were preserved (1905 Pacific no. 152 has been restored and run extensively since the mid-1980s); sadly not one M-1 was spared for later generations to appreciate so handsome and clean-lined a locomotive and tender.

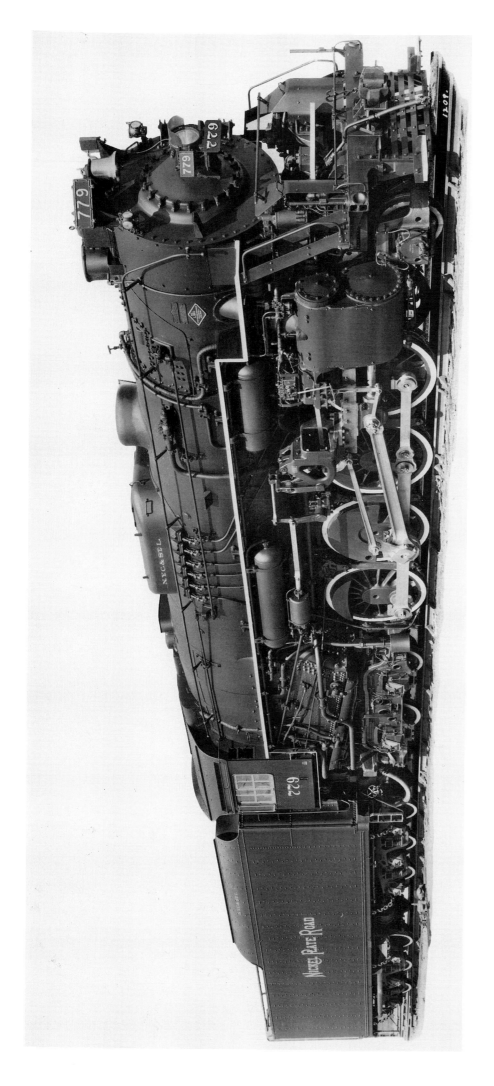

126

Nickel Plate Road
No. 779

The last of eighty 2–8–4 Berkshire types constructed by the Lima Locomotive Works in Lima, Ohio, for the Nickel Plate Road between 1934 and 1949 was the final steam locomotive to be built by that renowned company. With dieselization under way, this fine example of the "super-power" concept (large firebox, high horsepower, enormous steam-generating capacity) ran for less than nine years before even NKP was totally dieselized. Capable of wheeling manifest freights at seventy miles per hour, these "Berks" were magnificent engines. Six were preserved, including the 779, which, appropriately, is displayed in Lima. Sister no. 759 was returned to excursion service in 1968–1972, and no. 765 has been running several times a year since it was completely overhauled in the mid-seventies, so this superb class of locomotive, unlike so many of its contemporaries, is far from being extinct.

GENERAL INDEX

INDEX OF LOCOMOTIVE
WHEEL ARRANGEMENTS